OUR AMAZING BIRDS

Our Amazing Birds

THE LITTLE-KNOWN FACTS ABOUT THEIR PRIVATE LIVES

BY ROBERT S. LEMMON FORMER MANAGING EDITOR OF *The Home Garden*

WITH 102 PAINTINGS IN BLACK AND WHITE BY DON R. ECKELBERRY

THE AMERICAN GARDEN GUILD AND

DOUBLEDAY & COMPANY, INC.

GARDEN CITY, NEW YORK

LIBRARY OF CONGRESS CATALOG CARD NUMBER 52–8068

COPYRIGHT, 1951, 1952, BY THE LITERARY GUILD OF AMERICA, INC.
ALL RIGHTS RESERVED
DESIGNED BY ALMA REESE CARDI AND CHARLES KAPLAN
COMPOSED AND BOUND BY COUNTRY LIFE PRESS, GARDEN CITY, N.Y.

For bird watchers of all ages everywhere

$\mathscr{F}$OREWORD

Many books, I suspect, receive their titles after they have been writ-ten. But *Our Amazing Birds* put the literary cart before the horse, in a manner of speaking, by being christened before a line of the story had been put on paper.

With approximately fifteen billion individual wild birds occupy-ing the lands or coastal waters of the United States and Canada during at least part of every year, there are innumerable details about them waiting to be revealed, many so astonishing as to verge on the incredible. No one volume could possibly catalog them all, yet a representative selection is surely feasible. Thus the book which is now before you was conceived as a sort of concise though read-able interpretation of some of those species which, for one or sev-eral reasons, can scarcely escape being called amazing. Many of them are common today in our country fields and dooryards, others occasional or found only in particular environments, while a few vanished long ago but left great fame behind them.

Once the birds themselves had written the title, the outline of the book was merely a typewritten list of 102 species which Don Eckelberry and I, both of us bird students since boyhood, agreed would fit the purpose we had in mind. From this start we moved on to the tone which we wanted the text and illustrations to strike, tossing our ideas back and forth until, in less time than you might expect, the mood of the finished book and how it should be developed became clear. Only then did the work of its actual production begin.

The text, of course, was the foundation of our project, so as quickly as I had a few chapters ready I would send copies of them to Don, usually with certain paragraphs indicated as possible illustration themes. He would read them, make his own notations, and at frequent intervals we would get together and merge our viewpoints into a mutually agreeable decision. In this fashion, step by step and meeting by meeting, we carried through the entire undertaking in a spirit of frank and friendly give-and-take, which, we hope, is reflected in the pages that follow.

And now here is the ultimate result: fivescore authentic bird character sketches, each with its own interpretive portrait. There is no planned pattern in their sequence, as every one is distinct in itself and may be read without reference to the others. In each you will find specific facts about nest, eggs, and range, but above and beyond these I hope you will discover an inkling of what would be called personality if the subject of the sketch were a human being. For birds are no nerveless automatons, moving along dull and monotonous courses. On the contrary, they are alert, resourceful, sentient creatures, superb in the quickness of their reactions, incredible in their instincts and adaptability to the conditions of the moment. Though probably without the power of reasoning and conscious thought, as we understand those terms, they nevertheless display many emotions comparable to ours and often behave as we might try to do were we in their places.

The great difference—and this is one of the amazing things about them that you will come upon as you read—is that they do it much, much better!

R. S. L.

8

$\mathscr{C}$ONTENTS

9

OUR AMAZING BIRDS

RUBY-THROATED HUMMINGBIRD

JEWELED HELICOPTER OF THE GARDEN

Though there are over five hundred different species of humming-birds, the only one you are likely to see east of Texas and the Rockies is the ruby-throat. Throughout the central and eastern portions of the United States this tiny creature, weighing but one tenth of an ounce, is at once the amazement and delight of everyone who knows and grows outdoor flowers, for it is the most bejeweled little living helicopter you can possibly imagine.

Ruby-throats come north from their winter home in lower Florida, the Gulf Coast, and Central America as early in the spring as there are enough open flowers to provide the combined nectar and tiny insects which constitute practically all of their natural menu. From then until early autumn you may see them at any time poised in mid-air as they thrust their long, needle-like bills deep into the blossom cups, darting from flower to flower with wing strokes so rapid that they merge into a half-seen, humming haze. The wee birds are

15

perfect masters of flight, moving up, down, sideways, or backward with equal ease, and even halting motionless in the air for as long as they want to. In direct flight they travel easily at sixty miles an hour, and their wingbeats often reach the incredible speed of seventy per second.

Though less than four inches long, the ruby-throat is an intrepid battler against any bird, regardless of size, that it thinks may be a potential enemy. Crows and hawks are its especial hates, and the darting, adroit attack, spearheaded by that needle-sharp bill, soon puts the biggest adversary to undignified flight.

Only the male hummer has the lovely throat patch which, when the light is right, glows an unbelievably lustrous ruby red; the female's throat and the rest of her under parts are a commonplace whitish color. Both sexes are predominantly green above, bronzy-tinged in the female.

Quite a number of birds go through interesting aerial maneuvers in the mating season, but the ruby-throat's effort to impress his intended wife is something very special. While the lady sits quietly on a twig, he zips up and down at terrific speed on the arc of a circle maybe twenty feet across, chippering excitedly in his squeaky, unmusical little voice.

A ruby-throat nest is quite as exquisite as its builders—a wee, lichen-covered cup of plant downs saddled on a more or less horizontal tree branch ten or more feet from the ground. It is the most fairy-like and appropriate cradle imaginable for the two little white eggs, but if you are lucky enough to see one of the old birds feeding the young after they hatch, you may wonder if the tiny parent has suddenly turned murderer. For, believe it or not, hummers feed their young by regurgitation, thrusting their long bills into the kids' throats and ejecting the mixture of minute insects, et cetera, which they themselves have previously swallowed and partially predigested.

Hummingbirds are an exclusively Western Hemisphere family, the vast majority being found only in the tropics. The Far Western portions of the United States have seventeen kinds in all, but east of the Rockies, as I have already said, the sole representative of the race is the incredible ruby-throat.

$\mathcal{G}$REAT $\mathcal{A}$UK

IT VANISHED LIKE THE DODO

What the larger penguin species are to the Antarctic, the great auk, standing nearly three feet tall, once was to the North Atlantic from the Arctic Circle southward as far as Massachusetts and Ireland. Both birds resembled each other in some respects, being black above and white below, incapable of flight because of their extremely small wings, but superb divers and underwater swimmers. But whereas the penguins still survive, the great auk is believed to have become extinct about 1844, the victim of relentless persecution by fishermen who raided its breeding islands for eggs and meat, by feather hunters seeking a substitute for eider down, and by unrestricted shooting. Today there are no more than eighty mounted specimens anywhere in the world, and about the same number of their five-inch, buffy, mottled eggs.

Not too much is known about the habits of this strange big diver, for detailed records in the days of its abundance were few and often unreliable. It was, of course, a colony nester, laid but a single egg, and, when on shore, walked or sat erect in much the same way a penguin does. It must have been a skilled underwater swimmer, probably able to catch any fish it went after as well as to escape most of the sharks and other big ocean predators that tried to gobble it. In this subsurface life it used feet as well as wings for propulsion, unlike the penguins, which swim underwater only with their wings and use their feet for steering.

The great auk was not, as many people believe, a truly Arctic bird. On the contrary, two of its most populous breeding areas were near Labrador and Newfoundland, and apparently considerable numbers of the birds used to spend the summer in the region of Cape Cod. It is believed, too, that a definite southward movement took place in the fall and winter, carrying a few of the birds even as far as Florida. It is problematical whether this was a true migration such as motivates so many of our flying birds or merely a following of some favorite food fish which sought warmer waters during the cold weather. In either case, it was an amazingly long distance to swim, for remember that the great auk was entirely unable to rise into the air.

The world has seen many instances of man's reckless destruction of other forms of life which surrounded him, but somehow the case of the great auk is particularly discreditable. That millions of such harmless, half-helpless birds should have been exterminated primarily to provide food for white men's stomachs and feather beds for them to sleep on is a far from pretty picture for us to acknowledge.

AMERICAN BITTERN

HIS LOVE SONG SOUNDS LIKE A PUMP

Many birds have a variety of popular names based on their characteristics, but few can match the picturesque aliases which people have attached to this strange-looking haunter of both fresh and salt-water marshes and river margins over most of North and Central America. Depending on where you are and whom you are talking to, you may hear it called bog-hen, stake-driver, dunk-a-do, meadow hen, thunder-pump, barrel-maker, plum pudd'n, Indian hen, or almost anything else fantastic. All are more or less descriptive of its appearance, haunts, or the weird noises which constitute the male's song.

Bitterns apparently fancy themselves as hermits, skulking deliberately among the rushes, cattails, and tall grasses of the boglands and seldom showing their stocky, brown-streaked selves unless forced to take wing by a very close approach. If you should surprise one in the open, it usually "freezes" by tightening its feathers, pointing its bill upward, and generally imitating a stump root or crooked

19

limb projecting above the mud. At such times you never would suspect it capable of the lightning thrust of spear-like bill and long neck by which it captures its favorite meals of fish, frogs, crawfish, snakes, mice, and sometimes large grasshoppers.

Bitterns don't have much to say for themselves except in the mating and nesting season, when the males go into their peculiar song-and-contortion act, the "love notes" part of which, sometimes audible for a quarter mile or more, has been likened to the driving of a stake or the operation of an old wooden pump. Few people have had a good view of this performance, because it normally occurs in the dense cover of the swamp, but an excellent eyewitness description has been recorded by Mr. Arthur J. Parker in Edward Howe Forbush's *Birds of Massachusetts and Other New England States:*

"The preliminary motions were each time the same; a forward (horizontal) thrust of the head with opened beak whereby air was gulped—the bill being audibly snapped upon each 'mouthful.' This swallowing motion would be repeated perhaps five or six times, and during the operation a strange swelling and contortion of the neck could be plainly seen—it was as if the bird had swallowed a large frog. There was a downward movement of the enlarged part of the neck. Then at once followed the explosive eruption of air—the *boom*—closely followed by the second sound, a clear syllable *ka,* like the stroke of a mallet on a stake. This second syllable gave the impression of being *vocal,* but we had no proof of that." During his act the bird sometimes raises the small tufts of pale, plumy feathers which develop on each shoulder during the mating season.

Bitterns build rather flat nests of grasses and reeds, usually on the ground or on mats of marsh vegetation. Their four to six eggs may vary in color from olive brown to pale olive buff. Incubation occupies at least a month and is thought to be managed entirely by the female.

These peculiar birds spend the winter from Virginia and lower Ohio south as far as Guatemala and Cuba, and come northward into New England as early as the middle of March. An occasional straggler may linger in the North until December, but most of them head for warmer climates in September and October.

$\mathscr{E}$ASTERN $\mathscr{B}$LUEBIRD

A YEAR-ROUND DELIGHT

Snow may still lie deep on the ground when you hear the first warbling of a bluebird in the orchard or on a roadside fence post. Few sounds in all Nature are so pleasantly rich and yet simple; none is more welcome as an advance signal that spring is not far away.

These famous cousins of the thrushes, sky blue above and white and chestnut brown below, are among the friendliest of American birds. They seem to like people, and prefer to raise their families in open farming country, in many suburban communities and villages, and other places where people come and go freely. One facility they always require is an enclosed spot for their nests, such as a tree cavity,

21

old woodpecker hole, or a man-made birdhouse. Given this, they will often set up housekeeping within a few yards of a house or even a busy modern highway.

The female takes over most of the work of building the substantial nest of grasses, rootlets, fine twigs, and a scattering of feathers inside the dark retreat, but once the four or five light blue or whitish eggs have been laid, her mate shares the job of incubating them and both parents work at gathering food for the young birds after they hatch. Often a second or even a third brood is raised after the first one has taken wing, and in such cases the male keeps an eye on his oldest offspring while his wife starts building the new nest.

Throughout their family-raising period both parents will fight valiantly to protect their home against seizure by the imported English sparrows and starlings, both of which frequently try to dispossess them. Indeed, these two foreign interlopers are such insistent enemies at this season that they have had much to do with the present scarcity of bluebirds in some areas. If you are a bluebird lover you can do much for your favorites by providing suitable nesting boxes and promptly ejecting all foreigners that happen to get there first. But there's little you can do about the bloodsucking flies that sometimes take a heavy toll of the nestlings, except to clean out each box thoroughly as soon as it has been vacated.

All through the spring the males keep up their cheerful warbling, the embodiment of goodheartedness and well-being. You realize, then, the reason for that time-honored expression, "the bluebird of happiness." But it is a different story in the late fall when, on the threshold of winter, the same bird drops his sweet, subdued *cheerily, cheerily* from the top of a stark November tree. I know of no other birdcall so nostalgic, apparently so filled with loneliness and regret that the hourglass of pleasant weather is running out.

By August the latest brood is on the wing, and soon the bluebirds begin to gather in flocks preparatory to going south. A few may spend the winter as far north as lower New England if there is an abundance of cedar and sumac berries to eat, but the majority go farther south—even to the Gulf Coast—where there is a better chance to find the insect meals of which they are especially fond.

ℬLACK-FOOTED 𝒜LBATROSS

SKY CRUISER OF THE PACIFIC

The Ancient Mariner had only one albatross, which was rather more than he and his shipmates could endure, as you will remember. Perhaps it is just as well that nobody told him there are thirteen species of these flying cruisers of the warm-water oceans, and that one kind nested by hundreds of thousands on one small group of islands in the Pacific no longer ago than 1909.

About the only albatross you are likely to see in North American coastal waters is the black-footed, a dusky-colored three-footer with saber-like wings that spread a good seven feet from tip to tip. Once seen (usually well offshore), you can never mistake it for even the largest-size gull, so distinctive are the shape and proportions of its wings and the manner in which they are used for apparently effortless gliding and banking.

The historic breeding grounds of the black-footed are the Marshall Islands, Midway, Laysan, and others in that general part of the Pacific. Here they gather in November to lay their single big eggs right on the ground, generally making a slight mound of earth with a depression on top to receive it. Incubation is so slow that often it is February before the young birds hatch out. Baby-sitting is a lengthy process too—a good six months of attention before the youngsters are able to fly and more or less look out for themselves. A few weeks later young and old take off for the open spaces of the Pacific, a vacation from family duties that continues until late the following autumn and may carry them as far as Alaska and the waters off the California and Mexico coasts.

For all their great size and power, albatrosses are gentle, trusting birds with comparatively little fear of mankind. For days at a time

they will follow ships at sea to garner whatever edible refuse is thrown overboard. Outside of this, their diet consists chiefly of such fish and jellyfish as they can catch themselves.

No doubt there would be far more albatrosses in the world today had it not been for the organized slaughter of the big birds for their feathers and fertilizer value which the Japanese carried on for many years prior to 1932. On one nesting island alone it is believed that the hunters murdered at least five million over the years, often with extreme cruelty, such as cutting off both wings and letting the birds bleed to death. Many of these were the white short-tailed species, now thought to be extinct. Happily, the black-footed is now protected by law and still nests in its age-old haunts on Midway and Laysan islands.

Despite their apparent dignity, albatrosses are rather comical characters when they strut and bow and croak in their courtship ceremonial dance. No doubt it is serious business to them, but people who have seen it report that to our eyes it is one of the most ludicrous performances known to birds.

Incidentally, the greatest bird wingspread in the world—eleven feet and probably more—is said to belong to the white wandering albatross. This may well have been the kind that the Ancient Mariner killed, but there are no authentic records of its ever being seen in our part of the world.

As a family, the albatrosses are splendid illustrations of bird adaptation to a highly specialized way of life. When you consider their size, and the vast over-water distances that they cover for months on end, it is obvious that they must be able to remain aloft with virtually no effort; hence the peculiar expanse and shape of their wings. Only the ocean, though, can supply them with food, and so they must have webbed feet capable of propelling them when they alight to eat or perhaps rest. Again, waterproof plumage is essential, and consequently albatross feathers are extremely oily. Even their colors and markings are unobtrusive in the open sky, in contrast with the intricate pattern of land birds which, like the sparrows, spend their lives amid leaves and twigs and grasses, whose general effect they must simulate to avoid detection.

$\mathcal{C}$ROW

SMARTEST OF OUR NATIVE BIRDS

Of all our native American birds, the crow has most thoroughly mastered the problem of how to thrive in the face of heavy odds. Tough, resourceful, amazingly intelligent, it prospers despite the handicaps of large size and a jet-black uniform which make it almost startlingly prominent. Man's hand is ever against it, yet it caws derisively and flaps away in safety almost every time. It is incredible the way crows make crime pay. And yet, if it's not your corn that has been stolen or your nestling robin that has been gobbled, you can't help admiring their skill and daring.

How does a crow manage so successfully that today its tribe is probably more numerous all over central and eastern North America than when the Pilgrims landed at Plymouth Rock? Well, for one thing, crows stand together against the world, helping each other on every possible occasion; so strong is their communal spirit that they even spend the night together in crowded flocks that may number fifty thousand birds or more. By means of variations in their far-carrying calls they signal the approach of danger, the discovery of food, the presence of natural enemies like foxes and large hawks and owls. When several are feeding together, a sentinel is detailed to stand guard in a nearby tree and sound a warning in crow language if its keen eyes detect anything suspicious. Again, their hardiness and power of flight and sight enable them to cover many miles of countryside every day and hunt out adequate supplies of food—animal or vegetable, it's all the same to them. Also they are astonishingly versatile in adapting themselves to changing conditions, and invariably they get up very, very early in the morning; often they will slip silently into your dooryard before the family is awake, steal fruit, vegetables, or any other tidbits they have spotted, and depart as silently and safely as they came. It is as though, living by their wits and faced by constant perils, they have perfected as their family slogan, "United we stand, divided we fall."

There is a perpetual argument among bird-informed people over whether the crow does more harm or good in the world. On the one side, it devours vast quantities of sizable insects in all stages of development, mice, rats, snakes, carrion of all kinds. On the other, crows rob other birds' nests of eggs and young, raid the poultry yard for the same purpose, gobble great amounts of the farmer's grain as it sprouts in the fields. Probably, in the broad picture, their evils just about match their good works, at least in the minds of those who accept the theory of checks and balances that governs all of Nature's plan.

Crows are migratory to the degree that in the northern part of their range only a corporal's guard remains during the winter months. Their southward drift, though, does not begin until late autumn, and the travelers return early in the spring so that their rough stick nests high in sizable trees are often occupied by four to eight bluish-green mottled eggs in mid-April. Over much of the breeding range there is only one brood a season.

Here, then, are a few highlights on an exceedingly smart bird. Perhaps Henry Ward Beecher gave us the best summation of this sable fellow's intelligence when he remarked that if men wore feathers and wings a very few of them would be clever enough to be crows.

$\mathscr{W}$ILLOW $\mathscr{P}$TARMIGAN

BROWN IN SUMMER, WHITE IN WINTER

Most birds wear their brightest colors in spring and summer and their dullest ones in the autumn and winter, but the willow ptarmigan reverses that fashion. All through the cold months it is snowy white except for a black tail. Then, as spring comes, it begins to turn black-barred chestnut brown around the head and neck, the change continuing downward until, in the case of the female, all the white has disappeared except on the densely feathered legs and feet and the expanded wings. Males go through a similar procedure, though retaining more white on the under part of the body.

29

The reason for these peculiar color alterations is really simple enough. These members of the grouse family are birds of the Arctic tundra, that weird, all but treeless land that stretches northward through Alaska, Banks Island, and central Greenland. Save for a short summer season, the earth is snow-covered there, and all land creatures that move about would be dangerously conspicuous in any color except white. Conversely, white could be seen at once when the browns of the earth reappear with returning warm weather, so a darker camouflage must be assumed for that season.

Ptarmigans have other oddities too. When mating time comes the males fight bitterly with each other and set up an amazing din of squawks and hoots—all because of the ladies. Most of the racket occurs between ten at night and two in the morning, the period of minimum daylight in the Far Northern spring and summer.

In other members of the fowl group such behavior often accompanies the ambition of each male to acquire a harem of several wives, but not so with the cock willow ptarmigan, which apparently covets no more than a single mate. So heavy is the fighting that only the strongest males win through to mates of their own, which may be a biological factor in a harsh, rugged land where only the fittest can long survive.

A ptarmigan nest is a simple affair of grass and feathers, built right on the ground. In it the hen bird lays from eight to a dozen buffy eggs heavily marked with dark brown. Curiously enough, this darker color can be easily washed off an egg that has just been laid, as though it were fresh paint. After some exposure to the air the "paint" hardens to the point of durability.

In summer these queer small grouse feed on both insects and vegetation, switching to berries in the fall and, in winter, to the buds and small twigs of dwarf willows and alders that huddle in the tundra gullies. This bud-eating habit seems to follow them in the southward migration which follows the nesting season and takes the birds as far as Sitka, the central Canadian Provinces, and even occasionally to the St. Lawrence. There are records of individuals crossing the border into our northernmost states, but they are very few and far between.

SLATE-COLORED JUNCO

AN OPTIMIST IN GRAY AND WHITE

From the tip of that stout little flesh-colored bill to the ends of the long white feathers which form the outer edges of its tail, the junco is every inch the "snowbird" so popular with millions of Americans from coast to coast and from the border to the Gulf. In spring it moves to breeding grounds among the hills and mountain ranges of Pennsylvania, New York, New England, and Canada, seeking a well-hidden nook on or near the ground for its deep cup nest of moss, bark shreds, and grasses in which to raise a family of four or five youngsters. But October finds it back on accustomed winter ranges, flitting busily among the weed patches, enlivening countless suburban yards and country farms with a welcome presence.

Slate gray or brownish gray above and white beneath, with a neat dark gray vest, the junco is at once trim and rugged, contented and restless. Snow, to it, is something to accept, to hop and flutter in, even to eat when ice locks the normal water sources. Certainly no snowy blanket is anything to be afraid of, but rather to be taken as a matter of course. There are always weeds and grasses rising above it, and their seeds are good eating. So are the grains and bread crumbs that people scatter on the crust outside the back door or spread on trays at their windows.

Toward the end of winter changed moods begin to show among the juncos. Often, on a warmish day, you will see them chasing each other wildly as if in play, diving and dodging through the air with startling agility and speed. Their sharp *chipping* calls continue, but

now and then the notes are run together into a little trill, monotonous, very earnest, almost pathetic in its plain simplicity. And then, in late March or April, you may be lucky enough to hear another junco song, part warble, part twitter, rambling but wholly pleasing. You might take this as a sort of farewell salute, if birds were guilty of such things, for very soon the "snowbirds" will start leaving for their nesting grounds, and by the time the apple blossoms open the last one has gone.

Actually there are several slightly different kinds of junco, all belonging to the same genus, in different parts of the country. The slate-colored is the common one in the East and westward across the Plains. In the mountains of the West there are the white-winged, the Oregon, the pink-sided, and the red-backed. But they are all "snowbirds" at heart, and perhaps that is what really counts most.

DIPPER

THE BIRD THAT TROTS UNDER WATER

The higher parts of our Far Western mountains, all the way from the Mexican border to northern Alaska, are the home of one of the oddest birds in this or any other land. Its body is no bigger than a robin's, yet it walks and flies as nonchalantly under water as above it, pays no heed to the coldest weather, and sings with equal cheerfulness in winter and in summer. Whether you choose to call it dipper or water ouzel, it is the same jolly little optimist in the waterproof gray feather coat, equally at home on the bottom of a swift-flowing mountain stream or teetering on a boulder beside it. And the dozen or so other members of its tribe, some in mountainous Europe, others in Mexico and down through the Andes to southern South America, are precisely similar in general character and predilection for watery homes.

The dipper feeds largely if not entirely on underwater insects, walking right down after them and trotting around on the bottom of the stream wherever the search may lead. At times it uses its wings quite casually to help its legs, and thereby makes surprising speed. Now and then the bird comes up for air, clambers among the boulders for a while with the peculiar dipping motion which inspired its name, and goes under again. In winter, when the stream surface is frozen, dippers utilize the occasional air holes, slipping down through one and up out of another with perfect indifference. At any moment they are likely to break into ringing, infectious song, suggestive at once of the mockingbird's and the house wren's.

Mountain water plays such an inseparable part in dipper life that the birds often build their nests right in the spray of cataracts, or even behind them where the only access is directly through the falling curtain. The nest itself is six or seven inches in diameter, more or less spherical in shape, and constructed of green moss strengthened with leaves, grass, twigs, and a bit of mud by way of cement. It has been said that if the location is not moist enough to keep the moss freshly green, the birds will spatter drops on it from their own wet wings. Customarily the location is among tree roots or in a rock crevice, and its only entrance is through a round hole just big enough for the parents to pass in and out. Altogether a perfect place to bring up three to seven children so they won't fear the water!

HOUSE WREN

A DYNAMO IN FEATHERS

This is the "Jenny wren" of household tradition, though why people should have pinned the feminine label on it is something of a mystery, unless they meant to imply that women are essentially fussbudgets who always find something to fume over. Personally, I'd

prefer "Jimmy" to "Jenny," for this brown scrap of energy and bubbling, irrepressible song strikes me as being a good deal more male than female.

There's just no stopping house wrens. Figuratively speaking, from the time they arrive from the South in April until the last one departs in October, there isn't a nook or cranny from Wisconsin to Indiana and Virginia to New Brunswick that they haven't poked into with their sharp bills and insatiable curiosity. During those six months they have chattered and sung enough bird words every day to fill a dozen unabridged dictionaries, consumed countless pounds of insects, built their twiggy nests in recesses that range from birdhouses and woodpecker holes to clothespin bags and fish baskets, and every pair has raised from one to three families of five to a dozen children each. On the side, so to speak, some of them have occasionally pecked holes in other birds' eggs, thrown a few young out of the nest, and otherwise made nuisances of themselves. But on the whole, no birds are more popular, widely known, and valuable in the over-all economy of Nature.

The family life of house wrens could fill a whole book and still be incompletely told. The first thing a male does in the spring is to sing. Then he starts building a nest in every suitable nook he can find. Later, when he marries, his wife looks over the spots he has chosen, selects one, and usually throws out all his sticks and brings in her own. She may change her mind, of course, and decide on a different home, but eventually the pair gets settled and the eggs are laid. While the female sits on them, her mate gallivants around the neighborhood, singing, chattering, chasing off other birds, building more nests just in case, and not infrequently teaming up with some unattached female and starting another family with her. Despite such flagrant lapses in fidelity, it is believed that some house wrens mate for life. Certainly there is no doubt that the males do their full share of bringing food for their insatiable offspring—quite a chore, when you realize that by actual count a single pair is known to have made six hundred food-carrying trips in a single day.

Sometimes, though, there is pathos in house wren life. I quote from a report sent to the late Dr. Edward Howe Forbush by Mrs. Daisy Dill Norton and published in his monumental work, *Birds of Massachusetts and Other New England States:*

"I wrote you this summer, in July, I think, about the female wren who took possession of the bluebird house and, with never the ghost of a father wren to support her theory of a family, went ahead building the nest and going through all the manifestations of a maternal wren with a family in prospect. She was around here until the end of August. She allowed no birds on her house or near her nest. She was ready to do battle with anything that appeared, regardless of size. In all those weeks we never saw another wren or heard the song of the male. This morning Dr. Norton took down the house. In the exquisitely built nest inside were twelve perfect eggs."

BOB-WHITE

FRIENDLY WAYS AND FAMILY TIES

Bob-whites are by far the friendliest and most engaging of our native fowl-like birds, lovers of the farm lands and orchards, grainfields and lush country meadows. Time was when the clear *bob-white* calls of the males rang out frequently from fence tops and low trees all the way from the Gulf Coast to Canada and from the Atlantic to Wyoming and South Dakota. Yet today, over many stretches of this great territory, you rarely if ever hear it, because the chunky little whistlers simply are not there.

This serious decrease in the bob-white population stems from a variety of causes. Chief among them, probably, is overshooting by steadily increasing numbers of hunters. Added to this are the losses caused by the severity of northern winters, a factor which, of course, was present even when the birds were extremely abundant a century ago. And finally, the changes in the physical character of their former breeding range in the Northern States resulting from the increasing density of human population, together with the increase of four-legged enemies such as cats and wandering dogs.

Bob-whites are rather trusting little fellows, normally sticking together in flocks or coveys, except during the spring and summer breeding season when they pair off and set up housekeeping on the ground under the shelter of thick grass tufts or brushy tangles. There is only one brood a year, but it may contain anywhere from six to eighteen or more youngsters hardly larger than big marbles when they break through their pure-white shells and start trotting about as soon as they dry off. Were it not for such customarily large families, the species could never have lasted even as well as it has.

If undisturbed, the parents stay with their young through the following fall and winter, the whole family roosting on the ground in a circle, tail to tail and each bird facing outward, so that if danger threatens they can all take off at top speed without getting in each other's way.

Tragically enough, this family trait of huddling together on the ground for the night sometimes leads to appalling losses by starvation. A heavy snow settling on the birds may cover them deeply, which in itself is no particular hardship. But if that snow should be followed by rain, and the rain by a sharp drop in temperature, most of the bob-whites in the storm area may be imprisoned under a vast icy crust through which they cannot peck their way to freedom before it is too late. There are innumerable records of whole coveys being found dead after such a crusted snow finally melts away; I have myself seen three such instances, and in each case all the bodies were in an area no more than a yard or so across.

Some states have passed total protection laws for bob-whites, with gratifying results, and it might well be that an enforced federal regulation along similar lines would restore this splendid bird to something approaching its former abundance, especially in the Middle and North Atlantic States. But unless and until that time comes, we can only hope that today's dwindling numbers of bob-whites are not slowly on their way to join the vanished ranks of the heath-hen and the passenger pigeon.

38

$\mathcal{T}$HE $\mathcal{E}$GRETS

THEIR BEAUTY WAS THEIR CURSE

These are the southern white herons whose snowy nuptial plumes, known as *aigrettes* in the shameful days of unrestricted millinery use of wild-bird plumage, had a market value as high as thirty-two dollars an ounce for use in women's hats and headdresses. So great was the demand for these ornaments that both the large American egret and the smaller snowy were brought to the verge of extinction by plume hunters before the Audubon Society was able to have official sanctuaries established for them and thus saved the day. Now, thanks to those early efforts against heavy odds and to an aroused public interest as well, both species are again on the increase.

Egrets are colony-nesting birds and breed in central and tropical North America, usually in wooded swamps and marshlands, where their stick nests are perched at various heights from bush tops to the taller trees. Many years ago both species apparently bred to some extent as far north as Oregon, Nebraska, and New Jersey, but that rarely happens today. If you want to see them busy with family life, you'd better go southward of Virginia. Once the young are on their own, though, many of the old birds wander during the summer into New England and occasionally as far as the Canadian border, apparently a sort of racial habit for which northern bird-watchers are eternally grateful!

Egret families are not large—only three to five eggs per pair, and not more than one brood a year. But what they lack in individual size they make up by community massing, so that a rookery at the height of the season is a very busy place indeed with its hundreds of nests and the incessant comings and goings and flappings and climbings which center around them. Frankly, it is generally odor-

39

ous as well as interesting, for young and old alike subsist mainly on fish, frogs, crawfish, and the like, and you know what hot, humid air can do to food like that. Frequently, too, an egg or a young bird drops accidentally to the ground and is never retrieved, which does not help the situation at all.

Whether flying, perching, or stalking slowly and sedately through shallow water in search of food, egrets are the essence of slender grace and beauty. Their plumage is as immaculate as it is snowy white, and the movements and poises of their long, slender necks alone are worth going far to see. There is about them an unbelievable elegance and air of refinement unmatched by any other native bird I know. We would lose much indeed were they ever to vanish from the American scene.

WHITE-THROATED SPARROW

LOVELY, LOVABLE, AND PERFECT SINGER

To hear the white-throat at its best, go to the evergreen country of the North in June. There, around the old clearings and open windfalls, the stillness will be broken at intervals by one of the loveliest of all bird songs, a series of fine, pensive, almost tremulous whistles, leisurely, dying away slightly toward the close. "Old, old Sam Peabody, Peabody, Peabody, Peabody" the singer seems to say, and the purity of his voice passes all belief.

It is largely across Canada and in our Border States, with some southward extensions into the mountain portions of New York, Pennsylvania, and New England, that the white-throats spend the summer and raise their two broods of four or five youngsters each. In late September they start moving south, often in small groups among which the young of the year are clearly distinguishable from their parents by the absence of clear white markings on head and

42

throat. Most of them continue to the latitude of lower Ohio and perhaps as far as Florida, but there are always some that linger all winter in southern New England, particularly where dense brush thickets and a good supply of weed seeds promise convenient shelter and food. One lone male, in superb adult plumage, haunted my Connecticut feeding station from last November until April, becoming surprisingly tame and never once deviating from the gentlemanly manners which seem to characterize his kind. He and the juncos were always the first to arrive for breakfast and the last to garner a final snack after sunset.

One of the most pleasant events in the white-throats' winter days is the sociable way a group of them will gather for the night in an accustomed sleeping retreat. Evergreen hedges are favorite spots, and here you will hear their distinctive *chinking* chorus as dusk begins. Sometimes, too, there will be a snatch of song, a mere echo of their summer melody but, like it, almost unearthly in its purity. And finally, with the coming of darkness, a keen ear may catch the low, companionable murmurings with which they settle down for the night.

$\mathscr{C}$EDAR $\mathscr{W}$AXWING

WINNER OF THE BEST-DRESSED MEDAL

Your first reaction to a good view of this sleek, crested, brown and
gray aristocrat with the black eye mask is that it is the best-dressed
bird in America. And as you become familiar with its ways you will
be quite sure to add that it is the best-mannered too.

Waxwings travel widely over Central and North America, including the lower tier of Canada, and you never know when or

where you will come across them. Theoretically they are migratory, but actually their movements are more in the nature of random wanderings with a tendency to drift southward in the fall and north in the spring. One year numbers of them may remain right through a tough New England or Midwestern winter, and the next they may disappear with the first frosts. Perhaps the uncertainty of their movements is linked in some way with the fact that they wait until late— June, July, and even August—before building their rough, bulky nests of bark strips, weed stems, rootlets, and so on fairly high in well-grown trees. In view of this delay you'd think that they would raise only one brood, but two seem to be common and there is even a record of three. Often September finds four or five very small youngsters still in the nest.

Genuine companionability is another cedar waxwing characteristic. The birds like to travel in groups, and where you find one there are almost sure to be several or many close by. Though they utter nothing that you could call a song, they are forever talking to each other in low, hissing, rather hoarse whispers, and sometimes several will sit in a close row on a branch and apparently amuse themselves by passing some choice bit of food from one to another.

One curious trait is their habit of literally stuffing themselves when they find some favorite food item—cherries, for example. On such occasions they may become almost too full to fly, and there are reports that waxwings overindulging in overripe wild berries have become virtually intoxicated by the fermenting juices. They by no means confine their diet to fruits, however, but consume vast quantities of insects. It has been conservatively estimated that a flock of thirty cedar waxwings will eat ninety thousand cankerworms in a month, plus no one knows how many other grubs and such. In those years when the destructive elm-leaf beetle is rampant you often see waxwings busy for hours in the trees, harvesting the ugly, spiny larvae from the under sides of the foliage.

All in all, the cedar waxwing is deservedly one of our best-loved birds. It seems to have more "social graces" than any other species (barring that appetite, of course!), and its invariable good looks and quiet, courteous ways are always engaging.

$\mathcal{M}$YRTLE $\mathcal{W}$ARBLER

OUR HARDIEST WOOD WARBLER

Like many others of our numerous warblers, the myrtle nests quite far north—in this case, the northern tier of states and on to central Canada and Labrador. But it differs sharply from most members of its family in being far more resistant to cold weather and perfectly capable of subsisting on a vegetal instead of an insect diet if circumstances point that way.

To a degree these two characteristics dovetail very neatly, for the plant foods that the myrtles particularly like are the fruits of the bayberry, which ripen in the fall and persist so far into the cold weather that many myrtles simply continue feasting on them all winter even as far north as the New England coast, where this shrub grows abundantly. It is always a surprise to see their blue-gray and white forms, with the yellow patch on the lower back which has earned them the alias of yellow-rump, flitting among the thickets in the midst of a bitter northern snowstorm. On occasion, too, they feed on berries of the cedar, woodbine, honeysuckle, mountain ash, and even poison ivy.

The myrtle warbler in winter is distributed literally from ocean to ocean and as far south as the Panama isthmus and the Greater Antilles. In the spring migration northward the males are especially showy in their heightened colors as they flutter among the branches, displaying to the full not only the rump patch hallmark but also the yellow crown and side splashes and the white markings on their outer tail feathers. Some other warblers are more gaudily dressed, but none except the redstart does so perfect a job of spreading out its nuptial wardrobe for all to see. As you see them flycatching

nimbly in the warming sunshine you can't avoid the conviction that they are among the handsomest of their famously bright-garbed tribe.

Myrtles like evergreen trees for housekeeping purposes, and there they build rather bulky nests (for warblers) with dried grasses, stems, bark shreds, and so on, generally bound together with spider-webs and lined with plant down or sometimes hair or feathers. It is usually late May or well into June before the first of the four or five white eggs spotted with brown and purplish has been laid and the female starts her two-week incubating job without even waiting to complete the laying part of her duties. Her mate gives her little help except the encouragement of his constant little trilling song, but she can always depend upon his being near at hand.

You might expect that so hardy a little bird would raise a second brood, but this the myrtles rarely if ever do. Perhaps the reason lies in the fact that, for some unexplained reason, the drift southward begins as early as the second half of August, and of course young as well as old must be ready for it.

$\mathscr{B}$ELTED $\mathscr{K}$INGFISHER

A PRIZE PACKAGE OF ODDITIES

Whatever way you take it, the kingfisher is an avian oddity. Big-headed, short-tailed, weak-footed, it looks like a tousled monstrosity, yet is an expert flier and diver, a fearless defender of home and fireside, and the last word in self-reliance. Though its chosen diet is fish, there are times when the bird turns eagerly to wild fruits and even grasshoppers. With it all, kingfisher life seems regulated by a set of fixed habits adhered to with surprising tenacity.

Human fisherman are supposed to be quiet folk, but this feathered master of the game often lets go with a rough, harsh cry which has been well likened to the sound of one of those wooden whirligig rattles that children swing so vigorously when they reach the real noisemaking stage. This is its invariable reaction to intrusion on its feeding grounds, but apparently it is also a frequent way of expressing irritation at missing a fish the bird had expected to catch.

A kingfisher has favorite fishing stations, too, which it uses with great regularity—a dead branch of a tree, a tall, bare post, a telegraph wire—almost any unobstructed perch overhanging or very close to either salt or fresh water. Here it will sit motionless, sharp eyes scanning the water for an unwary fish venturing too near the surface. Then, at the opportune moment, it plunges headfirst, often going completely under water and, if luck is good, emerging with a minnow or other small fish firmly gripped in a strong, oversize bill. At other times it will simply fly along over the water until, sighting a meal, it halts, hovers briefly, and then dives like an arrow.

Don Eckelberry

Kingfishers are rather solitary, lone-wolf birds, except in the spring, when they mate and begin digging the long tunnels in which their new families will be housed. The customary site is a steep, bare-faced sandy or gravelly bank, usually near water, and near the top of it both birds join in excavating a four-inch burrow that runs in quite horizontally for three to fifteen feet and, at the end, is enlarged considerably to provide room for nesting. The old birds use their bills for digging and their feet for removal of the loosened soil; the whole job may mean from two to ten days of hard work. Ultimately, five to a dozen white eggs are laid on a crude flooring of fishbones, scales, twigs, leaves, et cetera, and if you are wise you won't go poking around the burrow when one of the old birds is at home, for you'd probably get a painful nip from an extremely capable bill.

Belted kingfishers are coast-to-coast birds and breed over a vast area from the southern United States to Alaska. In winter some of them migrate as far as Colombia and the West Indies, while others remain as far north as Ohio and upper New England.

$\mathcal{G}$ROUND $\mathcal{D}$OVE

TINIEST OF OUR PIGEONS

Much as the "chippy" is the companionable little dooryard bird of the North, so the ground dove fills that role in the Southern States from South Carolina down through the coastal plain and low country generally into Florida and on westward to Texas. Hardly larger than a good-sized sparrow, chunky and gray and neat, it walks and trots contentedly across the lawn, through the garden, along the dusty roadside paths, nodding its head as it goes, and often singularly undisturbed by your human presence. Its voice is as simple and well-mannered as its appearance and ways—a soft *woo-oo, woo-oo, woo-oo* repeated over and over until you wonder, quite without criticism, why the bird never tries to vary it.

These friendly little doves are primarily vegetarians, and the quantity of weed seeds they consume must be enormous, for they seem to spend most of their time looking for them. In this, as at most other times, they seem supremely gentle, but on occasion they unhesitatingly go after other birds seeking the same food, and may even row a bit among themselves. Even these outbursts have an element of dove-like courtesy in them, and it is doubtful if much damage is ever done to any of the parties involved.

Ground dove nests are not unlike those built by others of the pigeon tribe—simple affairs of grass, twigs, and maybe pine needles, in which two plain white eggs are laid. Their breeding season may extend as long as seven months; the late T. Gilbert Pearson, one of our great ornithologists, records having found nests with fresh eggs in Florida as early as February 28 and as late as September 26. Dr. Pearson noted another curious fact, based on extensive observation: while the early spring nests were usually built on the tops of rotted stumps, the later ones were on the ground in grainfields or weed patches, or sometimes among the fronds of palmetto trees. Still later, in July, August, and September, practically all the working nests were located on the larger boughs of orange trees or the horizontal supports put up to hold the sprawling scuppernong grapevines. As many as four broods a year are raised, and it is said that the parent birds mate for life.

All bird-watchers have their favorite species, and the ground dove is certainly one of mine, as it quite surely will be one of yours if it has the chance. There is no escaping its trimness, courtesy, and devotion to its own quiet affairs. And there is no more exquisite tracery in all Nature than the embroidery trails left by those busy feet trotting this way and that across the clean, dry cloth of sand in the scrub country that ground doves love so well.

$\mathcal{R}$ED-WINGED $\mathcal{B}$LACKBIRD

SLEEK DANDY OF THE MARSHES

Some mild, spring-tinged day in late February or early March the word that winter is over comes from the roadside marsh in the rich, throaty *con-ka-reee* of a male redwing's song. Against the pale tans and grays of the countryside his jet-black form stands out sharply as

52

he perches in a bush top or sentinel tree, though not until he flies to another post are you likely to glimpse the startlingly brilliant, buff-edged shoulder patches which give him his name.

Days pass, and the first advance scout from the South is joined by others and still others until the wetlands are vibrant with their unmistakable voices. All of these early comers are males, and soon they form into flocks which range the countryside, often gathering by dozens in treetops to stage a ten-minute chorus that has no parallel in all bird life. Not until the females, migrating northward a few weeks later, have joined them in some numbers do the flocks break up as mating gets under way. And with that event begins the second spectacular phase of the redwing's year as the males, seemingly proud of their shining black uniforms and scarlet epaulets, vie with each other in bowing, spreading their wings and tails, displaying all their manliness to impress the dusky, comparatively Quakerish ladies.

Eventually matches are made and the pairs scatter to build their woven grass and cattail nests, each to hold four or five eggs, among the sedges, tussocks, or bushes of the fresh-water marshes. Family life there seems singularly free of dissensions, despite the fact that several pairs often settle in the same smallish swamp or meadow. The males stand watchful guard near the nests, alert to drive away marauding crows and other natural enemies, even lodging bold and noisy protests if a human being approaches too closely. Fussing with neighboring families rarely occurs, for each seems to respect the others' territories. By our standards, redwing moralities do have their flaws, for one male may have two or even three devoted wives. But, again unlike the human race, there are no jealousies!

This favorite blackbird is very widely distributed, breeding from Nova Scotia to Alaska and southward to Florida, the Gulf Coast, and central Mexico. It is one of our most useful birds, too, for it destroys untold multitudes of insect pests. The one mark against the bird is its injury to some grain crops, particularly in the West and South when, in vast, almost militarily maneuvering flocks, it moves down across the country in its fall migration. But the good far exceeds the bad, as is the case with virtually all of our native birds.

CALIFORNIA QUAIL

BLACK COCKADE AND FANCY FACE

Bird-watchers with active imaginations could be forgiven for calling this chunky Westerner the drum-major quail, or something like that, because of the black forward-arching cockade crest and the unique black and white face pattern below it. Indeed, there is more than a suggestion of the military about the bird's whole bearing and in the brown, slate-blue, and tawny uniform it wears.

You are bound to like the California or valley quail on sight. Active, fast-running, and always alert, it is also a strong flier and an excellent conversationalist. One of its frequent calls is a sort of three-syllable crow, and others have been described as *kuk-kuk-ka* and *coo-coo-coo*. Also, male birds say *kerk* with great authority when their mates have eggs in the nest.

These true quails are found from southern Oregon down through California, except in the large deserts, where their place is taken by the somewhat similar Gambel's quail. They are sociable birds, often gathering in sizable flocks during the non-breeding season; under these conditions, especially, you will generally see a single one apparently standing watch on a post or other observation spot, ready to warn of approaching danger. Where they are not molested they become quite tame and come readily to feeding stations. Primarily they are seed- and insect-eaters.

Gallinaceous or fowl-like birds are ground nesters, and the valley quail is no exception to the rule; its grass-lined nest is built in a slight hollow where it is somewhat sheltered by bushes, a brush heap, rock, or old fence. The family trait of having many offspring is followed too, a typical clutch containing as many as a dozen or fifteen creamy-white or brownish eggs spotted with red-gold. The lady of the house attends to the hatching while her man stands guard near by. You could not ask for cuter kids when they finally escape from their shells and start scuttling about like wee striped mechanical toys. At this stage they are covered with down instead of regular feathers, but each has a tiny topknot in imitation of Pop's and Mom's.

$\mathscr{S}$NOWY $\mathscr{O}$WL

VISITING GIANT FROM THE FROZEN NORTH

About every four years, with impressive regularity, the United States as far south as the Carolinas and northern Texas are invaded by thousands of huge pale birds that move on utterly silent wings spreading as much as five feet from tip to tip. They are the famous snowy owls, fresh from the Arctic North—some of them even from as far as land is known to exist—because of food shortage (largely

among the lemmings, which are subject to serious periodical epidemics). Sometimes the first ones arrive as early as October, and it may be well into April before the last depart. But meanwhile, as in the winter of 1949–50, even the big city newspapers run stories about them, so great is the public interest in their presence.

The snowy owl deserves its fame if ever a bird did. Its size is spectacular and so is its color, largely pure white with some barring of brown or grayish on the upper parts. Further, it hunts more by day than at night, so it is visible far away. Again, both males and the larger females are distinctive, almost hawk-like, in their vigorous manner of flight, and their perching spots are usually in the full open.

While with us, the snowy owl is a silent bird, despite its ability to sound a deep, hoarse croak as well as a shrill whistle. You are most likely to find one in open, frequently treeless country, perched on a post or even a high point of ground as it watches for moving rabbits, rats, or mice, sometimes catching a duck on the wing or even snatching a fish from nearby waters. Seashore marshes and dunes are particularly favored haunts, and once a snowy has found a territory to its liking it is apt to remain in it until the time comes to head northward again. Occasionally an individual bird will allow you to approach within fifty yards before taking flight, and that will be a red-letter day indeed, especially if you have binoculars to bring vividly to you the beauty of the penciled markings, the legs and feet feathered to the toe tips as protection against the cold, and the wild glare of those big yellow eyes staring straight at you.

Back again in their Arctic homeland, which actually is circumpolar, the snowies start nesting as early as the first of June, for the season is short and time must not be wasted. The sites they choose are merely high points in the rolling tundra, where they scrape out a slight depression in the soil to hold their four to ten pure-white eggs. Most birds wait until the last egg has been laid before starting incubation, but not these big owls. No sooner does the female lay the initial one than she begins sitting on it, with the result that the first young bird may be almost ready to fly by the time the last one emerges from its shell.

$\mathcal{C}$ATBIRD

A VARIETY SHOW THAT NEVER FLAGS

Ornithologically speaking, the catbird is one of the Mimidae family —in plain English, the Mimic Birds. As a group, they have a great deal to say, and say it in a wide variety of ways. Some, including the mockingbird and the brown thrasher, introduced elsewhere in this book, are among the finest bird mimics in the world.

This slim, long-tailed, slate-gray fellow with the darker tail and topnot is a friendly, inquisitive, and endlessly amusing character who seems to enjoy living near people. It is forever flicking about in the shrubbery, splashing vigorously in the birdbath, hunting for grubs on the lawn, striking comical attitudes and changing instantly to others. Vocally, it is just as versatile and seems to take equal pride in mewing like a cat and singing disjointedly a hodgepodge collection of notes and phrases impossible to describe. You never quite know what a catbird will do next, but you can always be sure it will be something different.

Catbirds breed throughout the area from Florida to Texas and northward as far as Nova Scotia, Quebec, and Manitoba. As we know them in the Middle and Northern States, though, they are only warm-weather visitors, usually arriving from the South in May and departing in October. But what entertainment they can crowd into those six months!

You might expect catbirds to be careless, irresponsible parents, but not at all. To begin with, their twiggy, rootlet-lined nests are substantially built, strongly supported, and astonishingly well concealed, usually in heavy shrubbery, vines, or densely foliaged trees. From the time the four or five greenish-blue eggs are laid in May until the young leave the nest, the mother bird, particularly, is unfailingly devoted to their care, and her mate is always near by to lend a hand if need be.

During this whole period both parents are the "watch-birds" of the neighborhood, setting up such commotion of mews and scolding chirps at the first hint of an approaching enemy that every other bird within earshot is alerted to defend its own. It is not unusual to see a prowling cat so rattled by a hastily assembled defense force of robins, song sparrows, orioles, and what have you that she goes right away from there. And it is usually the catbirds that sounded the first warning and led the counterattack.

Only once have I known catbirds to look disconsolate. That was when a pair of them nested in a forsythia bush a few yards from our kitchen door and lost every egg to a marauding jay just after the last one had been laid. For a few hours both birds acted as though they had no further interest in life. But the next morning they were hard at work making a fresh start in a different location.

No, you just can't keep a good catbird down for very long!

60

ℬOBOLINK

THE BIRD WITH A DUAL PERSONALITY

Judged by human standards, the male bobolink is a bird of dual personality. In May and June, a harlequin in black, buff, and white, he fills the air above lush, sunlit meadows with an indescribable jumble of rollicking, jingly song—first to impress that soberly dressed lady in the grass below and later, when he has won her and a family is under way in a well-concealed nest on the ground, apparently from the sheer joy of living. More often than not he pours out his song while on the wing, almost as though the pent-up volume of it kept him air-borne. Yet he does not resort to voice alone to win a mate, for at times, if you are a good bird-watcher, you will see him following her about on the ground, dragging his spread tail pigeonwise, partly opening his wings and raising his buff neck feathers like a ruff.

Despite all this gaiety, though, the bobolink is a good and faithful husband, mounting guard near by while the five or six mottled eggs are being incubated, calling a warning if he sights an intruder, and driving or luring away all that he can. After the young hatch, he calms down amazingly and does his full share of feeding the new family; if he were a man, you'd be sure to comment on how seriously he took his paternal duties.

The other side of his double personality comes to the fore in July, when, the single yearly brood having learned to shift for itself, the parent birds idle about the country as the mood strikes them. At this season both males and females change their dress, the former discarding all spring finery in favor of their mates' sober garb, and the females becoming even less noticeable than before. You hear no more singing now—merely an occasional *chink* dropped from the summer sky, pleasantly clear but a shade nostalgic.

By mid-August young and old alike have left the high country and are congregating in the river marshes and other lowlands, gradually drifting southward until by the middle of September vast flocks have assembled in the South Carolina rice fields, where they feast on the ripening grain and become so fat that men call them butter-birds. This is the great rallying region upon which all the bobolinks converge, whether from the Central States, New England, or British Columbia. And it is from here that they all move southward through Florida to take off for their winter haunts in southern Brazil, Argentina, Bolivia, and Paraguay, some via Yucatan and Central America, some by way of Puerto Rico and the Lesser Antilles, and the rest across Jamaica.

A long journey indeed, but they'll be back again next spring in hundreds of thousands, all entering the United States through Florida and fanning out northward and westward for another busy season among pleasant fields.

$\mathcal{F}$RANKLIN'S $\mathcal{G}$ULL

A WATER BIRD THAT LIKES DRY LAND

If you are accustomed to thinking of gulls as birds of the coastal waters and open ocean, this pretty little species with the white under parts and slaty mantle and head will come as a real surprise, for it is as typical of our Prairie States as are the cattle or the boundless distances. In spring, when the land is being plowed, thousands of these "prairie pigeons," as the ranchers call them, follow almost at the workers' heels, gobbling every grub and worm they find. And later, when the young are on the wing, you will see vast flocks fairly whitening the dry flatlands or winging gracefully across the sky in unforgettable beauty.

Franklin's gull is essentially an insect eater and consequently of great value in a region so beset with cutworms, grasshoppers, and other plant pests. Even in the nesting season it remains far from large bodies of water, preferring marshy lakes and sloughs. Often such places are crowded in late May with hundreds of semi-floating nests built of dead reeds and rushes, many within a yard or two of each other, carrying two or three dull white, brown-blotched eggs apiece. The downy youngsters pop overboard almost as soon as they hatch, and paddle about unconcernedly like so many animated little

powder puffs. With the old birds wheeling overhead or floating buoyantly on the water, the whole site of the colony presents a picture that will never fade.

The mass flocks of spring are repeated on an even greater scale in late summer and early fall when the gulls are preparing to start the southward migration which will carry them as far as the Louisiana and Texan Gulf Coast and even down the Central American isthmus through Panama and so to Peru. In the Dakotas, toward the end of August, I have seen thousands in one such flying army; the entire sky was thickly dotted with their flickering white forms.

This is not the species, incidentally, which saved the Mormons' crops from hordes of black crickets in 1848–50 and is now commemorated by a monument in Salt Lake City. The heroes of that occasion were California gulls, a much larger kind whose territory is the West Coast and the inland areas adjacent to it.

$\mathcal{B}$ALTIMORE $\mathcal{O}$RIOLE

HE WEARS THE COLORS OF A LORD

Tradition has it that the Baltimore part of this gorgeous orange and black fellow's name was given to it by the famous naturalist Linnaeus in honor of Lord Baltimore, whose family colors the male bird wears. Be that as it may, many a country boy knows it as firehangbird or perhaps golden robin—the former obviously because of the flaming hue of much of the plumage coupled with the characteristic pendent nest, and the latter probably on account of the male's loud song, which faintly suggests a robin's.

About the time the oak trees begin to leaf out in the Southern States these cheerful open-country birds arrive from their winter sojourn in southern Mexico, Central America, and Colombia. First come the males, many of them pressing northward as far as the Canadian Provinces, others lingering so that breeding time finds the species distributed east of the Rockies from South Carolina and Texas to the border and beyond. And wherever they settle, the flash of their plumage and the ring of their clear, rounded whistling underscore the welcome news that "the orioles are back!"

Birds of the trees, they are—big, comfortable shade trees such as elms, maples, oaks, and even large apples. First thing you know, they have mated, after much posturing and display of plumage beauty by the males. Then, each pair having selected its own territory, work begins on those wonderfully woven pear-shaped nests swung from drooping branch tips high above the lawn or even directly over a heavily traveled highway. Plant fibers, moss, hair, bits of soft string, yarn, fabrics—out of these the female, with only her beak for a needle, fashions a structure so durable that often the last remnants of it still cling to the supporting twigs three or four years after its service ends. Her mate seldom lends a helping bill, but he is always near by, watching her progress and seeming to whistle constant approval and encouragement. Interestingly enough, only materials of inconspicuous colors are selected; many tests have shown that where pieces of variously colored yarn were hung in convenient places these orioles always picked out the white and pale gray ones in preference to reds, greens, or other bright hues.

The ingenuity of the construction is as amazing as it is practical. First a number of long strands are hung over the twigs to serve as framework, and then the bird loops and weaves them intricately together. In three or four days she has the outer form of the pouch completed, and soon the inside lining is finished and the laying of the four or five eggs begins. The lady Baltimore does nearly all the incubating, too, and apparently she appreciates her lord's nearby singing, for she sometimes answers him from where she sits inside the nest. Finally, when hatching day arrives, the male assumes his full share of bringing up the new family without for a moment relaxing his vigilance (and, if necessary, battle) to keep all possible enemies at a safe distance.

66

$\mathcal{P}$ETRELS

SEA BIRDS OF MYSTERY

If you have ever crossed the Atlantic or the Pacific by ship, you may have seen, perhaps hundreds of miles from the nearest land, flocks of little blackish birds skimming low and fast over the water, following the contours of the ground swell and often touching the crests lightly with their feet in passing. These are one or another of the petrel species—probably either Leach's or Wilson's—the famous "Mother Carey's chickens," as many sailors call them, or sometimes "stormy petrels," because even mid-ocean blows seem to count for little in their strange way of life. Of these two wide-ranging species, the former breeds on islands off the North Pacific and North Atlantic coasts and migrates southward below the Equator as cold weather approaches, while the latter reverses the procedure by nesting in the Antarctic during our winter and coming northward as far as Labrador in our spring and summer months.

Petrels are among the oddest of birds. They nest in often thickly populated colonies, Leach's digging burrows in the soil a few inches in diameter and two or three feet long, while Wilson's chooses rock crevices or sometimes a hollow which it fashions itself. The actual nests are nothing to boast about, for they vary from zero to a few pebbles or bits of grass, feathers, twigs, or rootlets. But a single egg is laid in a season, and apparently the male incubates it during the daytime while his mate is off foraging far over the sea. Then, as night closes in, the females return, relieving the menfolk, who promptly take off for the wide open spaces, where they spend the hours of darkness. Apparently petrels can see equally well by day as by night, a rare gift among birds. After the nesting season is over they literally live at sea, feeding on a variety of tiny marine creatures and sleeping on the water when the mood strikes them.

A petrel colony is a weird, ghostly place at night. The birds have little fear of man then, constantly coming and going as they "change the guard," and keeping up a chorus of soft coos, chuckles, and squeaks, apparently the accepted form of greeting between incomers and outgoers.

It is small wonder that generations of superstitious seafaring men have held these amazing martin-size birds in awe, considering them as symbols of coming storms, wrecks, and kindred deep-water disasters. Nor is their eeriness entirely a matter of sailors' imaginations, as witness a passage in the late Edward Howe Forbush's highly authentic book, *Birds of Massachusetts and Other New England States*. Writing of Leach's petrel, Dr. Forbush says:

"Our observations during the cruise of the *Avocet* seemed to prove that birds several times the size of the petrels have a strange, unaccountable fear of them. We took a petrel from its warm burrow in daylight and released it. It flew at once to the ocean, going toward a great flock of clamorous herring gulls sitting on a ledge near the island. Immediately every gull ceased its cries, took wing, and fled silently out to sea. Later we released petrels on other islands on which gulls or terns were breeding, and however numerous or clamorous were the birds immediately about us, the appearance of a petrel on the wing silenced their cries and caused a local exodus. No one has been able to account for this, so far as I know, and it may not be a universal experience; but it was ours."

$\mathscr{I}$NDIGO $\mathscr{B}$UNTING

TROPIC BRILLIANCE BY NORTHERN WAYSIDES

To bird-watchers from the Gulf States northward to Minnesota and the lower portions of the Canadian Provinces this venturesome little finch comes each spring like a winged message from the Central American and Panamanian tropics where it has spent the winter. A male in his full breeding plumage seems as exotic as something out of the *Arabian Nights*—a vigorous little tad in intense indigo blue, changing to green or even blackish with every shift of light.

Arriving only with the really warm spring days, and starting to drift southward with their companions as early as September, the male indigo buntings are not only among the most colorful of our smaller birds, but impressive singers as well. Right through the hottest hours of June and July, and sometimes even in August, you will hear their cheery *swee-swee-swee, swee-swee, sweet-sweet-sweet, swee-swee* again and again from favorite telegraph wire or treetop perches. A simple little song, with its alternately higher and lower phrases, but one of which you never tire.

When a male indigo courts a soberly brown female he does it largely with song, following her hour after hour with hardly a pause in his serenade. Naturally enough, the nesting season is governed by the latitude rather than by the calendar. In Virginia, for example, the eggs are generally laid between late May and the middle of June; the customary time in Massachusetts is ten days or so later, and it may be well into July before pairs that settle in Maine complete their twig, grass, and leaf nests a few feet from the ground in bushy pastures, brier patches, and similar tangly places.

Sometimes two clutches of three or four eggs each are laid, and most of the incubating chore devolves on the lady, while her husband spends his time singing not far away, except for an occasional relief trick on the nest. He leaves most of the feeding program to the mother bird, too, but when the youngsters are nearly ready to fly he tapers off on his singing and takes a bit more interest in family affairs. Like most brilliantly colored birds, his autumn and winter costume is much duller—almost as brown as the female's. Sometimes the same nest is used for a second brood, and there are records of its even being repaired and used again the following year, a decidedly unusual bird procedure.

Indigo bunting food is chiefly insects, but many weed seeds are eaten too. One of the prettiest sights of sunny May days is two or three brilliant males feeding on the fluffy white seed heads of dandelions dotted over the lawn.

Common Tern

MASTERPIECE OF STREAMLINED GRACE

There are seventeen species of the tern tribe found in North America, and you could search a long time to find sizable birds of any kind that can match them for grace of flight and all-around agility in the air. Superficially, most of them suggest little, slender gulls, but their tails are long and forked, their flight is more buoyant, and when in the air their bills often point downward instead of being held more or less horizontal. The characteristic color scheme at maturity is white below, pearl gray above, and a black cap on the head. Some people call them sea swallows, because of their graceful flight—a well-deserved compliment. One species, the arctic tern, makes probably the longest migrational journeys known, from its summer nesting grounds in northern Canada and Greenland to a winter range as far south as the Antarctic Ocean.

Several kinds breed and summer along the Atlantic Coast from the Carolinas northward, including the common tern. This is the species you are most likely to see through much of this area, and also inland on large bodies of fresh water, especially the Great Lakes and other regions west and south.

A common tern nest is nothing to boast about architecturally—usually hardly more than a depression among the sand, pebbles and shell debris along the beach, but occasionally quite a mound of seaweed, grass, and so on. There is only one brood a year, normally consisting of only two or three eggs, but both parents are extremely devoted to their project and share the incubation and other chores.

Perhaps the most interesting phase of common tern home life is the birds' habit of nesting in colonies of many pairs, usually on an island where the danger from prowling animal enemies is minimized. Often the nests are only a yard or so apart, and as the young birds begin wandering around almost as soon as they hatch, the problem of lost children would seem to be a perpetual headache. As far as the kids themselves are concerned, they really do become thoroughly lost, but in some miraculous manner the right parents always manage to locate the right youngsters and fill them up with fresh fish. In such a colony the air is full of parents coming with food or going for more, and as their children are constantly hopping and dancing about, and the returning parents calling as they come in with food, the general tumult is something to see and hear. Apparently each arriving bird recognizes its offspring from the air, so there is a certain amount of orderly results despite the chaos.

Later, when the young can fly a bit, they head for the shore and begin to learn to catch their own food. Unlike many of the land birds, this is a slow process; maybe tern brains take a while to wake up. Be that as it may, it is far from unusual to see a parent passing food to a husky, strong-flying child while both are on the wing, or bringing it to him while he sits passively on the water.

Screech Owl

A WAILING VOICE IN THE NIGHT

Traditionally, owls are supposed to say *to-whit, to-who,* or *hoot-hoot,* or something like that. But the screech owl does nothing of the sort, nor does it screech. As a matter of fact, its usual speech is a low-pitched, tremulous wail, half whistle and half voice, often so long-

drawn that many superstitious people in the South call the bird "shivering owl." But to thousands and thousands of bird-watchers throughout eastern North America it is one of the most welcome of all night sounds, replete with the mystery of darkness and the noise-less sweep of soft-feathered wings from tree to tree while other birds are soundless and asleep.

Screech owls are little fellows, somewhat shorter than robins but normally appearing much stouter because of their big round heads, stubby tails, and rather loose, soft feathers. Like other birds of prey, they are meat eaters, living very largely on mice, large insects such as grasshoppers, cicadas, and night-flying moths, and a scattering of miscellaneous small creatures such as lizards, spiders, crawfish, and occasionally a bird. Very definitely they are beneficial to mankind through their destruction of crop pests, as indeed are practically all of our owls and hawks.

You could hardly ask for a more friendly bird. In the days when country and suburban houses were large and ornamented with an assortment of filigreed copings and cornices, screech owls often slept among these recesses during the day and even nested there. Old orchards and ancient shade trees around the house are still favorite homesites, for here the birds are likely to find the sort of limb cavities they like as hiding places for the four or five white eggs that the female lays sometime in April or early May. On occasion, too, they will choose a nest box made especially for them, particularly if it is somewhat naturalistic in appearance.

There is only one brood a year, and the eggs take three weeks or so to hatch. By the time the youngsters are on the wing it is early summer, and suddenly the newspapers begin carrying stories about people being savagely attacked at night on the street or in their own dooryards by unseen, fearsome demons that beat them over the head and snip them with scissors and generally carry on like imps straight out of purgatory. If the authors of these tales knew birds as well as they do typewriters, there'd be no mystery to write about, for the explanation is perfectly simple: it's merely a pair of screech owls defending their young and, quite naturally, trying to drive away creatures that they think might harm the kids. In this they are as bold as they are sincere, and while their attack generally consists of nothing more dangerous than bill-snapping and sweeping dives that miss you by inches, they sometimes do actually strike your head and inflict some scratches, as I know by personal experience.

Oddly enough, some screech owls wear an over-all reddish color scheme, while others are gray. The actual markings are the same in both cases, and as yet there is no real explanation for this hit-or-miss distinction among individuals which are otherwise identical.

The screech owl is not migratory in the usual sense of that term, but the chances are that there is some seasonal movement whereby birds nesting in northern parts of the range drift a little southward in winter. Broadly speaking, though, the species is a year-round resident wherever you find it.

AMERICAN FLAMINGO

GORGEOUS IN COLOR, INCREDIBLE IN HABITS

Man and his civilization being what they are, the lot of the American flamingo has not been an entirely happy one. For one thing, this great vermilion bird, with its black wings, fantastically long legs and neck, and strangely shaped bill, is so shy that it will nest only in very remote spots, and then where conditions are favorable for establishing the unique mud-nest "cities" to which it is partial. Furthermore, its only known natural food is a particular kind of small shellfish, which still further limits its distribution. And finally, young flamingos are such excellent eating that, until strict laws were passed to protect the species, human raids on the few breeding colonies seriously decimated their numbers.

Flamingos are purely tropical birds and have rarely been recorded north of Miami, Florida. Probably none now breed in the wild any-

77

where within the United States, and in recent years their nesting numbers even in remote parts of the Bahama Islands and other parts of the West Indies have dwindled. A group of them kept at Hialeah race track, in Florida, furnishes about the only chance most of us have to see one alive, but it is good news that a hitherto-unknown colony estimated at thirty-five hundred was discovered not long ago on the Yucatan coast by an expedition from the National Audubon Society.

Flamingo life in spring centers around their unique breeding "towns" located on the flats beside open salt-water lagoons. Here, with their grotesque "upside-down" bills, each pair scoops up the mud and pats it into a conical pile about a foot high and twice as wide at the bottom, leaving a shallow, unlined depression on top in which a single white egg is laid. During the four weeks required for incubation both birds share the duty of keeping it warm, and both, it is thought, divide the feeding of the downy white chick by regurgitation after it emerges from the shell.

Infant flamingos are restless little rascals, quite the opposite of their dignified elders. When only a day or two old they think nothing of scrambling out of the nest and trotting around the colony, returning apparently when their parents call them to be fed. Each old bird seems to recognize its own offspring, and if the wrong youngster tries to scramble back into a nest he will get a tweak with a huge bill to warn him that he's entering the wrong pew.

The feeding technique of a flamingo is one of its strangest oddities. Standing on its straight, stilt-like legs, the bird lowers its head until the bill, *upside down,* is in the mud. Contrary to the usual rule, the lower mandible or "jaw" is immovable, while the upper one does the moving. Thus, while the flamingo stands figuratively on its head, the heavy upper mandible chomps up and down against the lower one, straining out the little shellfish from the mud in which they live.

A flock of flamingos striding along in close ranks presents a peculiarly soldier-like appearance. And when, for some reason, they break into the clarion honking which is their customary call, the military illusion is complete.

$\mathscr{S}$CISSOR-TAILED $\mathscr{F}$LYCATCHER

THE SKY IS ITS TRAPEZE

Down in Texas, Oklahoma, Kansas, and adjacent areas they often call this exotic beauty the bird of paradise and eagerly watch for it to arrive in spring from a winter sojourn in Central America. It is by far the most striking of the whole flycatcher tribe, a delightful blend of soft grays, rose, and black, topped off with a little crown patch of orange-red and, most amazing of all, a deeply forked tail whose two flowing feather streamers are sometimes ten inches long—more than half of their wearer's total length. As if these characteristics were not amazing enough, the scissor-tail is a superb aerial gymnast much given to seemingly impossible sky dances and acrobatics.

Scissor-tails are as gay in manner as in dress, yet they seem to find particular satisfaction in driving away such heavyweights as crows, hawks, and vultures which they think might have designs on those five creamy, spotted eggs in the bulky nests of plant stems, weeds, cotton, and so on, which they build a few yards from the ground or sometimes on the crossarms of telegraph poles. In such cases their attacks are fearless and devastating; often they actually light on their victim's back and hammer away at him with their very capable bills.

Their antics in the air are incredibly graceful and unexpected. One favorite maneuver is a series of swift climbs and dives whose rapid succession is made still more spectacular by the spreading and closing of the long tail feathers. At the top of each climb the bird gives a harsh scream, for no apparent reason except the pure joy of being so alive. Another trick is to fly along slowly in a straight line and suddenly shoot upward with a shriek. Were the birds not so obviously capable and sure of themselves you might think them scatterbrained if not actually "touched in the head."

Where people are concerned, the scissor-tail is decidedly on the friendly side, often nesting close to houses and generally frequenting open spaces such as man prefers. You often see them perched on wires, fences, and dead branches after the fashion of less spectacular flycatchers, and not infrequently several pairs will nest a good deal nearer each other than you would expect from such high-spirited birds.

Of course scissor-tail food consists almost exclusively of insects, and there is one odd fact about it: the preferred diet is crickets, grasshoppers, beetles, and weevils, rather than the more lightly built flies, butterflies, and so on. A very high percentage of the total consists of injurious species, so the bird is a very practical as well as theoretical friend of the human race.

$\mathcal{B}$ARRED $\mathcal{O}$WL

QUEER COMEDIAN WITH SOLEMN EYES

All owls are a little on the weird side—not merely because of their appearance, but also in their ways. But somewhere in the ancestry of the barred owl there must have been a prince of clowns, and his influence still crops up in some of the most ludicrous ways to be found in the bird world.

Ordinarily these seriocomic characters express themselves in orthodox owl hootings, but on occasion two or three of them go on a sort

of conversational spree with no holds barred, jabbering away at each other with such an amazing jargon of *wha-whas, ow-ows,* and *ya-yas,* intermixed with cackles, catcalls, and half screams, that you wonder if they have gone out of their minds. Yet it all seems to be merely an act into which they sometimes go on slight provocation. Often I have started them at it merely by doing a bit of *wha-wha-ing* myself in a heavily wooded region such as they frequent. Once this happened toward dusk of a gray December day, when the two genuine owls involved in our three-way powwow were clearly visible in the bare trees no more than fifty yards away. I never saw a more ludicrous bird performance, for the ridiculous clatter was accompanied by equally madcap posturings. Maybe they were mocking me as I was them—who knows?

Barred owls are widely distributed through middle and eastern North America from the Gulf Coast north to Manitoba and Newfoundland. To a degree they are migratory, those in the more northerly parts of the range moving somewhat southward as winter nears, but not carrying through to really distant parts. They nest early, too —sometimes even in late February—though they undertake only one brood a year. Frequently the nest, with its two or three white eggs, is located in a large tree cavity; sometimes the site is the abandoned nest of a gray squirrel, crow, or one of the large hawks.

Like nearly all of our native owls, the barred lives largely on mice and other small mammals, supplemented with large insects, frogs, and now and then a bird. Practically all its hunting is done at night, and its flight is as silent as a breath because of the amazingly soft, almost muffled texture of its wing-feather webs. Should you catch a glimpse of one in flight you would be struck by the apparent shortness of its wings and their measured yet graceful beat.

Yes, the barred owl is quite an individualist. You don't really know it, though, until you have heard the diabolical scream with which it occasionally startles every living creature within hearing distance. It is the most maniacal night sound I know, and it rips through the darkness with bloodcurdling suddenness. How strange that it should come from a bird with such dark, solemn, and almost humanly expressive eyes!

CHIMNEY SWIFT

A FLICKERING MISSILE IN THE SUMMER SKY

This stiff-winged, sooty-colored little speedster is doubly well
named, for it nests in chimneys and flies faster than perhaps any
other of our birds. Any day, from April to October, you are likely to
see swifts zipping around the sky after insects, their curved, flickering wings and projectile-like bodies immediately suggesting bent
bows with arrows on the strings. Perhaps the unverified estimate
that one of them flies a thousand miles in an ordinary summer day
is not too far from fact. One wonders how quickly they cover their
autumn journey to the Amazon basin in Brazil and back again in

the early days of spring. During the spring and summer months you may see them almost anywhere in eastern and middle North America as far west as the Rockies.

Chimney swifts are even odder in habits than in appearance. Their nesting places are the insides of hollow trees and unused chimneys, where, in semidarkness, they attach their shallow twig nests to the vertical walls with a glue-like saliva from special glands in the builders' mouths. The construction starts with the cementing of a few twigs to the chimney walls, then the addition of others to them until the nest is completed, in perhaps eighteen days. Each dead twig is broken from some tree branch by the swift flying against it and grasping it in bill or feet—a slow process which is chiefly responsible for the time required to complete the job. Often the first of the four to six white eggs is laid before the building operation ends, and the parents, taking turns, can settle down to the duty of incubation.

Toward the latter part of summer, especially, chimney swifts sometimes roost in swarms in the broad chimneys of large buildings, entering them at nightfall by the simple procedure of raising their wings above their backs and dropping straight down. Inside, they cling to the wall with their feet, using their peculiar spiny tail feathers as props. Audubon, the famous ornithologist of the last century, records that he once estimated the number of swifts assembled thus in a huge hollow tree at nine thousand, ranged in tiers around the cavity, with the first arrivals nearest the top.

Except when asleep or sitting on their eggs, chimney swifts spend practically their entire lives on the wing; courtship and even actual mating taking place while in flight. They take to the air in early morning and do not leave it until dark, even riding out thunderstorms and heavy gales which drive all other birds to cover. Hawks mean little or nothing in their lives, for they are supremely confident of their amazing gift for speed.

Darkness seems to be the one adverse condition which they heed, and if it should come unexpectedly, as occasionally happens when an exceptionally black thunderstorm is making up on a summer afternoon, they are likely to retire to their chimneys as if real night were at hand.

$\mathscr{T}$HE $\mathscr{P}$HALAROPES

THEIR LADIES WEAR THE FAMILY PANTS

Somewhere away back in the mists of early phalarope history a company of gremlins must have had a wonderful time turning established bird customs topsy-turvy. Ever since that hypothetical day these odd little feathered characters have been doing things differently. At least that might be a layman's explanation of the facts that phalaropes look like sandpipers but have duck-like feathers and spend much of their time swimming far out at sea; that the females always wear the pants in the family; and that their husbands never gripe about playing the role of the perfect Caspar Milquetoast.

There are only three species in this peculiar family—the red, the northern, and Wilson's. The first two breed in the Far North from Alaska to Greenland and probably spend the winter out at sea as far south as the Falkland Islands. The red's migrations are chiefly along the Pacific and Atlantic coasts, while the northern may be seen in migration throughout the United States, Mexico, Central America, and even Hawaii. Wilson's phalarope, on the other hand, is satisfied with less distant nesting grounds, breeding from Washington to Alberta and southward into California, Colorado, and the Midwest, and wintering from Chile and central Argentina to the Falkland Islands. Of the three species this is perhaps the most inland form. The northern is only six and a half to eight inches in over-all length, the red measures seven and a half to nine inches, and Wilson's is the largest—eight and a half to ten inches.

As I have said, a female phalarope wears the pants in the family. She is larger than her mate, boasts a brighter and more strongly marked dress, and even takes the lead when it comes to courtship proceedings. Husband phalarope, on the other hand, builds the nest

85

(often merely a depression in the soil, gravel, or moss), incubates the three to six greenish eggs after friend wife has laid them, and looks after the youngsters. Once she has done her family duty by producing the eggs, the lady figuratively washes her wings of the whole affair and goes off gallivanting by herself. Actually she may not come home at all unless she hears her mate's alarm call, indicating that some danger threatens the nest. Under such circumstances she will usually return and help him to defend the new family.

This may sound as though the females are a bit Amazonian in temperament, but in point of fact all phalaropes are rather gentle, trusting birds and you could not possibly liken the females to bullies. Both sexes trot about lightly on land, fly swiftly, and swim buoyantly with their long, slim legs and lobed feet, often spinning about like tops on the water while they gather food from it. Their meals consist mainly of marine worms, little fish, insects (including mosquitoes), and various tiny marine creatures such as whales feed on. This last diet item leads to their common name of "whale-bird" among the market fishermen and also gives a clue to their rating as real blue-water birds.

$\mathcal{T}$RUMPETER $\mathcal{S}$WAN

SNOWY GIANT WITH A MIGHTY VOICE

Time was when this great white bird with the clarion voice nested in the Middle West, the Plains States, and the Pacific Coast, but that was many years ago. Today, about the only places you are likely to see it are in Yellowstone Park or on certain lakes in Montana, unless you are fortunate enough some spring to glimpse and hear a small flock heading for some unknown nesting rendezvous in the wilderness of the Far North.

It must have been thrilling, in the days of the trumpeter's vanished abundance, to see the V-shaped flocks of these huge snowy birds sweeping southward in the fall and hear their bugle calls approaching and then dying away in the distance. They are over five feet long, when their necks are fully extended, and proportionately broad— much larger than the whistling swan, our other native member of the family, and nearly twice the size of our familiar Canada goose. They are said to be the highest fliers of all our waterfowl, migrating at even greater altitudes than the cranes, yet their size and color make them almost startlingly visible in the sunlight. Even today, in their tragically reduced numbers, they are one of the most magnificent sights of the American bird world.

Trumpeters nest on open ground, usually on knolls near water, where they construct piles of dead grass, weeds, feathers, and down. About a half-dozen dull white eggs comprise their normal complement, and both parents are such formidable defenders of their treasures that even the larger predators think twice before venturing within reach of either bill or wing blow. As with all swans, their food consists chiefly of vegetation gathered below the surface of fairly shallow water by the simple processes of submerging their heads and long necks and pulling it up.

The decimation of these superb feathered giants, which once nested in vast numbers from our northern states clear up to Hudson Bay and the Arctic Ocean, is a story of destruction all too familiar in wildlife history. The birds' conspicuous size and color made them the target of every hunter who could get within range. Too, there was a lively traffic in swan's-down, particularly on the northern breeding grounds, and since the hunters who followed it were without scruples where a chance for money was concerned, innumerable nestings were broken up when the slaughter of the old birds left the eggs or helpless youngsters to be eaten by any wolves or foxes that came that way. Records of the Hudson's Bay Company tell only too clearly the speed of the destruction. Around the year 1840 one post traded in some five hundred swanskins annually, mostly trumpeters, and another post handled about three hundred. Between 1854 and 1877 the yearly number sold by the company dropped from 1,312 to 122. And so it went.

𝒞AROLINA 𝒫ARAKEET

OUR ONLY EASTERN AMERICAN PARROT

There are well over five hundred species of parrots, but only one, the subject of this sketch, is known to have lived and bred in the United States. I use the past tense advisedly, for this gorgeous orange, yellow, and green bird, once abundant along the Atlantic coastal plain from Virginia to southern Florida and also from the Midwest down to the Gulf Coast, is now believed to be extinct. Color, habits, edibility, destructiveness to many cultivated crops—all those characteristics combined to doom it at the hands of the white man with his gun. By the 1880s none could be found except in very sparsely settled areas.

Carolina parakeets were not large, as parrots go—only about a foot long over all. But they were hardier than others of their tribe, and stayed year round even in the northern parts of their range. They were unsuspicious of people, too, and are said to have become fully tame within a few days after being caged, as many of them were. One of their great handicaps in the face of persecution was their devotion to each other which apparently influenced them to live in flocks, except during the breeding season, and certainly led to the death of large numbers which kept returning to the same spot where some of their companions had just been shot.

Carolinas, like most parrots, probably mated for life. Their nest sites were holes in trees, where they laid three or four white eggs. Little is known of the details of incubation and young-raising, but it has been established that the old birds fed largely on fruits, many kinds of seeds and grains, and nuts such as pecans and beechnuts.

Those of us who are familiar with parrots only as cage birds are unaware that in the wild state they are exceedingly strong, swift fliers. The Carolina parakeet was no exception to this family fact; on the wing it was as speedy and graceful as any dove, and exceedingly agile in dodging through the forested river bottoms which it so often frequented. It was a conversational sort of bird, too, and a flock busy dissecting thistle seeds, a favorite food, kept up a running fire of low, half-articulate sounds. Another frequent note was described as a sharp, rolling call.

If there are any Carolina parakeets alive today, their most likely location would be in the heart of some Southern swamp wilderness. But none have been sighted for years, even by experienced observers who have searched diligently for them; so we may as well accept their disappearance from the earth as an accomplished fact.

$\mathcal{P}$INE $\mathcal{G}$ROSBEAK

WANDERER FROM THE NORTHLAND

Just as the male evening grosbeak presents an over-all color effect of black and greenish yellow, so is the larger but closely related pine grosbeak a masterpiece in black and rosy red. The ranges of both species as well as their erratic migration habits are quite similar, too, though the pine is the more easterly of the two—in the spruce forests of northern and northwestern Canada and northern New England for the breeding season, and irregularly southward in winter to the Midwest and Middle Atlantic States. The exact causes for these occasionally wholesale population shifts of the two birds are somewhat obscure, for they are perfectly able to withstand the cold of the Far North if other factors are favorable. The general opinion is that periodic food shortages are at the bottom of the situation.

Pine grosbeaks are true wilderness birds, nesting usually in conifers and raising their three to four young in complete seclusion. Many of them are so unaccustomed to man that when they visit us in winter you can approach them closely before they become alarmed. On several occasions small flocks of them feeding on climbing honeysuckle berries paid no attention to me until I was no more than a yard away, and once I was able to catch one in my hands.

They are handsomely rugged-looking, robin-size birds with noticeably round heads and shortish necks, and their clearly whistled *tee-tee-tew* call note is pleasant and far-carrying. The full song, seldom heard except on their breeding grounds, is a cheery blend of trills and warbles, given with evident zest and enjoyment. Sometimes you hear snatches of it even in midwinter when the mercury is flirting with the zero mark.

Deep snows are no handicap to pine grosbeak life, for the birds' chief foods are the seeds, fruits, and buds of trees which not even a record blizzard can bury. Indeed, they actually welcome a good fall of flakes, bathing and fluttering in them much as less hardy characters do in water. The sight of several individuals sprucing up in this way, sometimes on the ground but often among evergreen branches where the snow has lodged thickly in the needle clusters, is a memorable highlight of any bird-watcher's experiences.

Ash seeds are one of their favorite dishes, and there is a record of a flock of around a hundred completely stripping a large, heavily laden tree in a single day. Various evergreen seeds are welcome, too, as are those of birches and larch, with a dash of weed seeds thrown in if opportunity offers. Practically all kinds of pulpy wild tree, vine, and shrub fruits make welcome fare, and bird-feeders will be glad to know that sunflower seeds are particularly alluring.

All birds from the Far North bring a certain exotic appeal with them when they wander down to visit us here in the States, but in the case of the pine grosbeak this subtle impression is especially evident. Part of it, I suppose, stems from their distinctive appearance, and part from the hardiness which marks their every action. And added to these vague clues is their outstanding *wintriness,* so marked that we seldom see them in any numbers before Christmas and rarely after early March.

$\mathcal{S}$NOW $\mathcal{B}$UNTING

FROM ARCTIC WASTES TO BATHING BEACHES

If, on a bitter wintry day along the New England ocean shore or inland where open farm lands give the wind full sweep, a flock of bluebird-size strangers whips past you, showing white under sides as they veer away and brown backs and black-tipped wings as they swing again in your direction, you can be quite sure they are snow buntings.

In view of their indifference to the blustering cold, you may not be surprised that these small visitors hail from beyond the tree line in the Arctic, very likely from northern Greenland, Grant Land, or the farthest reaches of Labrador. There, in summer, they build their nests of dead grass, moss, and plant stalks lined with fur or feathers, always on the ground or among rocks, and usually hidden in tussocks, crevices, or under large stones. A rugged life for little birds, but the four to eight eggs hatch quite normally in June or July, and by the time the blizzards come the youngsters are fully able to accompany their parents on the long journey southward.

Coming from such a background, it is no more than natural that we see snow buntings only in the most open kinds of country. The ground is their accustomed haunt for both feeding and sleeping, for back home they never saw a real tree and never think of alighting in one when they go traveling. Occasionally a barn or house roof will tempt a few to pause briefly, but not often. So apparently barren of

94

food are the ocean beaches, dunes, and inland fields which they frequent that one wonders how they can find enough to keep them hale
and hearty. But there they are, trotting about cheerfully among the
drifts of seaweed or occasional grass and weed clumps, garnering
seeds, tiny crustaceans, insects, and the like, each one intent upon its
own affairs but all taking to the air as one bird if something frightens
them.

In New England the arrival of snow buntings in large numbers
during October and November is considered evidence that heavy
snows and ice have covered their food supply in the Far North and
that we are in for a tough winter too. The first of these assumptions
is doubtless true, but the second is open to question since, with us,
the birds are often seen during an open winter. Every year a few appear south of the border, not only along the upper Atlantic Coast but
westward through the northern tier of states to the Pacific. But the
arrival of large flocks is problematical indeed; if they fail to put in
an appearance, we can safely conclude that the Arctic winter has
turned out to be not so tough, after all, and so the snow buntings are
making out all right up there. Perhaps it's a bit rough on them, but
many bird-watchers in the States rather wish that the weatherman
in the Far North would crack down hard every year!

PILEATED WOODPECKER

TREE CHOPPER EXTRAORDINARY

Strikingly patterned in white upon a solid blackish background, a
vivid red cockade topping a jaunty, long-necked head—such could
be a thumbnail sketch of this biggest American woodpecker, with
the single exception of the virtually extinct ivory-billed. Some call it
log-cock, and others cock-of-the-woods, both names derived from
its preference for the tall timber. Nowadays this forest habit seems

to be a little changed, for in certain areas the birds are seen with increasing frequency in more open country.

The pileated is a big bird, a good six inches longer than a flicker and with a wingspread ten inches or so greater. You may meet with one at any time of the year east of the Rockies from the low Canadian Provinces down to Florida and the Gulf Coast, as well as on the West Coast, for the species is only slightly migratory. And when that day does come, you are not likely to forget it!

True to the traditions of their tribe, pileateds are great choppers into decaying tree trunks and limbs, in search of their insect-grub food, and when they hit they make the chips really fly. Often they pry as well as chop with their big bills, quickly littering the ground with the debris from their work. The late Dr. T. Gilbert Pearson is on record as having once found a combination chip and splinter more than fourteen inches long beneath a tree where one of these birds had been busy. Not infrequently they cut rectangular feeding holes six or seven inches across and nearly as deep.

The courtship of these spectacular birds is a fantastic display of spread-eagling, crest-raising, dancing and bowing by male and female alike, interspersed with short circling flights as if to display their flashing white markings to the greatest advantage.

Like all good woodpeckers, a pileated pair chops a nesting cavity out of a dead tree trunk, whanging away until they have a hole from one to two feet or more deep and provided with a top entrance three or four inches across. In this retreat the lady lays three to six white eggs that are surprisingly small for such a large bird—actually only an inch to an inch and a half long. It is thought that she and her husband share the responsibility of hatching them, but evidence on this score is none too definite. This much we do know, however: both parent birds are publicity-shy during the whole nest-building and rearing season, and maintain discreet silence and secretiveness around the home neighborhood. Unless you are a careful observer and familiar with their ways, you may never find the nest at all, especially as it may be fifty or sixty feet from the ground. Numerous chips on the ground below are one of the best clues to its location, despite the fact that a good many are carried away by their carpenters.

$\mathscr{S}$CARLET $\mathscr{T}$ANAGER

BURNISHED BLACK AND BLAZING RED

No North American bird is more brilliantly colored than the glow-ing scarlet and jet-black male of this tanager species, and few can bring the thrill you feel when you see one clearly for the first time. Whether he is high in a tree, flying across a country road ahead of you, or feeding briefly on your own front lawn, you cannot escape the impression that a literal fragment of the fabulous Tropics has just flashed into view.

Actually the tanager tribe is predominantly a tropical group, and a large one. Of the three hundred-odd species, all confined to the

New World, only five are found in North America: the western, hepatic, and Cooper's on the West Coast, the summer tanager in the lower Central and Southern States, and the scarlet, whose breeding range is from the southern Canadian Provinces to South Carolina and Arkansas, with Colombia, Bolivia, and Peru as a winter resort.

Scarlet tanagers are real warm-weather birds and seldom put in their springtime appearance until the trees are well in leaf. As with so many birds, the males arrive first, sometimes in considerable numbers. Even this late in the season a cold northeast storm can so numb them and the insects which comprise their diet that many become so nearly helpless that they alight on the ground in all sorts of odd places, including open roads and suburban sidewalks. If the storm persists for two or three days, some of them succumb to cold and hunger, and in some areas many are killed by cars on the highways.

Normally, scarlet tanagers spend most of their time well up in the trees, where the thick foliage, coupled with their rather deliberate movements, makes them quite difficult to see. The males are great singers, though, and their jolly caroling, faintly rough when near by, can be heard for a long distance. They are one of the few birds that have the gift of ventriloquism, which makes the problem of locating the concealed singer still more difficult.

It is early summer before these fantastic birds set about raising their one annual brood of four or five, in a sizable thin nest of twigs, grass, and rootlets well out on a horizontal branch usually about twenty feet from the ground. The female, soberly dressed in unobtrusive yellowish green and dusky gray, takes over the whole task of incubation, for her brilliant mate would be far too noticeable for such secretive work. But he pitches into the feeding job with a will as soon as the young hatch, and altogether is a thoroughly devoted husband and father.

By early October the whole tanager family is on the way south, and at this time you can scarcely tell the old male from the female and young, for his gorgeous springtime red has been exchanged for an imitation of their inconspicuous traveling dress. Not until late winter will he regain his brightness in preparation for another season of showing us Northerners what the Tropics can do when they try.

CARDINAL

THE STATE BIRD OF KENTUCKY

Say "Kentucky cardinal" to someone from the lower Midwest, or "red-bird" to a Virginian or a Carolinian, and you will start a flow of praise beside which an Englishman's enthusiasm for the skylark would sound like a mere whisper. And that is quite as it should be, for this sturdy black and vermilion beauty is a bird in a thousand, a combination of character, color, and musical ability that merits top billing in any feathered company anywhere.

For one thing, cardinals are friendly, choosing by preference cultivated lands and coming freely right into your dooryard. The males' striking uniforms are fully matched by the vigor and clarity of their varied whistles—*whoit, whoit, whoit, whorty, whorty,* and so on; even the somewhat less daringly plumaged females are no mean singers, an unusual accomplishment in the bird world. For still another asset, you are likely to hear a cardinal singing any month in the year, even when the ground is deeply snow-covered.

The territory of this truly outstanding bird is principally from Florida, Alabama, and Texas up into the Midwest, and northward through the Atlantic States to New Jersey and lower New York. There are numerous though scattered records of its appearance in New England, too, and even some in Ontario. In recent years these occurrences have increased to a point which justifies the belief that the species is gradually extending its range northeastward as another Southerner, the turkey vulture, also has done. Regardless of where you find them, though, cardinals are likely to be year-round residents.

A male cardinal is a nearly model husband, following his mate and singing while she builds her rough twig and grass nest in tree, vine, or bush, bringing food to her while she incubates the three or four blotched eggs, and taking care of the youngsters for a while after they can fly, thus leaving her free to start a second brood.

From mankind's standpoint, cardinals are as useful as they are handsome, for one quarter of their food consists of insects (chiefly harmful to plants), and the balance is divided between weed and other seeds, and wild fruits. They do, indeed, feed to some extent on grain crops, but authorities estimate that the good they do is fifteen times greater than the harm.

This varied diet, too, makes them ready guests at home-grounds feeding stations, where countless people learn to know them well at close range. Many a depressing winter day is brightened by their vigorous, up-and-coming presence and the gaity of their fantastic garb. Year in and year out, they are morale-builders of the first water.

ℋOODED ℳERGANSER

HANDSOME ARISTOCRAT AND PERFECT PARENT

It is in early spring that you begin to see this showy little duck at its best on the quiet fresh-water streams and ponds over much of North America from the Gulf Coast to central Canada. This is the courting time, and the males, resplendent in fresh black, white, and cinnamon brown, are flashing their fan-shaped crests, posturing and rushing about in the water as they vie with each other in impressing the more sober and apparently indifferent ladies in the case. Later, when the pairs have settled in their summer homes on secluded, usually woods-surrounded waters, the feverish activity of the early season has gone, but in its place has come a docility and charm quite as appealing and equally fetching to the eye. In all the bird world there is no more charming a sight than a pair of hoodeds convoying their brood of eight or ten wee ducklings on the clear water of a forest lake, often with several of the little ones riding with evident enjoyment on their mother's back.

Like the wood duck, hooded mergansers nest in tree cavities often high above the ground and solve the problem of getting the youngsters down to earth by carrying them one by one in their bills or inducing them to leave the nest under their own power and scramble, flutter, or tumble harmlessly to the ground or water below. This commonly occurs soon after the eggs hatch, and from then on the ducklings can swim, dive, and rustle their own food like veterans. Only the power of flight is denied them until their wing feathers are well grown toward the end of summer, but meanwhile their busy webbed feet and the never-failing water roads serve them very well indeed.

In this country we have three species of merganser, of which the hooded is the smallest and, on the whole, the least numerous. Like its cousins, it has a narrow, unduck-like bill, equipped with many small serrations to enable it to catch and hold small fish without slipping. Along with this, of course, goes great expertness in diving and swimming under water, but for some reason the hoodeds are not as dependent on an actual fish diet as are the American and redbreasted mergansers, the other two kinds. Close observations indicate that they turn readily to small frogs, insects, seeds, and water-plant roots, and can get along without fish for many days if need be.

The hooded migrates from the northern portions of its breeding range in autumn, but many individuals winter no farther south than the Midwest and lower New England. Its beauty and rather unsuspicious nature are perhaps its greatest handicaps, for both make it a ready target for gunners. It may be that this is a primary cause for the scarcity of the species today compared to what it was years ago.

$\mathscr{E}$VENING $\mathscr{G}$ROSBEAK

FUNNY-FACED BUT FULL OF CHARACTER

This spectacular starling-size finch inevitably reminds you of a circus clown, especially when you see it for the first time. Showily clad in yellow, white, and black, broad of body and short of tail, it climaxes a harlequin appearance by possessing a fantastically stout, oversize beak of pale greenish yellow that would be the envy of any false-face maker. Even its actions are often clown-like, as when it seeks to frighten another bird from the feeding place by lowering its head, opening its mouth wide, and glaring balefully at the intruder.

104

Originally this rugged individualist seems to have been entirely a bird of the Canadian conifer forests from the Great Lakes into the Far Northwest. Early ornithologists, seeing it there, called it "evening" grosbeak because they thought it sang only late in the day—a limitation which certainly does not apply now. About 1890, though, a series of irregular mass movements eastward carried large numbers of the birds almost to the Atlantic Coast, so that nowadays the species is fairly common in winter through upper New York and New England and, occasionally, south as far as Maryland and Kentucky. When spring comes these visitors move west again, perhaps in a sort of misdirected migration at variance with the customary north-and-south flow of other birds. In any event, the result has been a greatly extended distribution, and opportunity for many more bird-watchers to become familiar with their odd appearance.

The winter of 1949–50 was a real "evening grosbeak year," and large numbers of them were seen in the lower New England and Middle Atlantic States. Usually they were in small flocks of three or four to a dozen or so, and in most cases they spent only a few days in one locality before moving on to another, as if they were on a sight-seeing tour. Their longest stops were where they found feeding stations plentifully stocked with sunflower seeds, and it was endlessly amusing to watch them deftly cracking this favorite food with their huge beaks, discarding the shells scornfully and swallowing the kernels with evident relish. It was comical, too, to see the apparent awe with which most of our regular winter birds eyed them when they first appeared; even the self-confident starlings treated them suspiciously, as if they were visitors from Mars. When this strangeness wore off, the usual rowings over food began, but the grosbeaks were a match for all comers.

Today this big, odd finch breeds from northern Michigan to British Columbia and south through the mountains to southern Mexico. True to its traditions, it prefers to nest well up in a spruce or other conifer, building a shallow cup of small twigs or rootlets in a dense needle cluster near the end of a branch. Only three or four eggs are laid—pretty blue-green ones lightly marked with brown, gray, and olive.

Wood Duck

SHOWIEST OF AMERICAN WATERFOWL

One does not think of a duck as being dainty and incredibly beautiful, but a wood duck drake in full spring plumage merits both of these terms. Blues, greens, purples, black, white, red, chestnut, and buff—these, with many gradations, are the chief colors of his stunningly striking and oriental feather pattern. Tone them down by half, or more, and you begin to approach the costume of his mate, a quite delightful little duck in her own right.

Wood ducks doubly deserve their name. Heavily wooded streams and ponds are their chosen haunts, and they have the odd habit of nesting in hollow trees anywhere from three to fifty feet above the ground or water. Sometimes they will accept a naturalistic man-made box in place of a natural cavity, but in any event the nest itself will be made of down, grasses, leaves, and other soft materials that make a comfortable bed indeed for the single clutch of eight to fourteen buffy-white eggs.

You may well wonder how the ducklings ever reach the ground or water from so high in the air within a few days after they hatch and while their wings are still wholly incapable of upholding them in flight. Arguments on this point have continued for many years, but the gist of the whole matter appears to be that they sometimes accomplish the feat under their own power and sometimes are carried on the back or in the bill of their mother. Wood ducklings' feet are provided with sharp, hooked claws, and their bill tips are similarly equipped, so that they can and do climb with ease. If the trunk of the nest tree leans, they often scramble down it backward; if it is more perpendicular, they are likely to flutter and tumble harmlessly to the ground when their mother calls them from below. In most cases where the parent carries them, the distance of the tree from the water seems to be the usual, but not infallible, reason.

Wood ducks are unlike the rest of their family in other ways too. For one thing, their customary call is not a quack, but a plaintive, whistled *oo-eek* by the female and a shrill little *peet* on the part of the drake. Again, when a pair is flying, the lady always leads the way, and at all times both sexes seem exceptionally gentle and well-mannered. Much of their food, in season, consists of acorns, for which they range the woodland floor not too far from water; a reliable survey shows that nine tenths of their diet is vegetal, with the remainder composed of insects and other animal matter.

A century ago this species was one of the most abundant of our fresh-water ducks, often nesting in the hollows of orchard and shade trees close to farmhouses. Persistent shooting by mankind, though, coupled with too much clearing of forest areas where they customarily bred, brought them so close to extinction early in the present century that rigid protective laws had to be enacted and enforced. Now, happily, the species is again increasing, so that you may find it breeding in suitable spots almost anywhere in temperate North America and wintering from southern British Columbia, Kansas, Illinois, Pennsylvania, and Connecticut southward to southern California, central Mexico, and the Gulf Coast.

$\mathscr{C}$OWBIRD

ALWAYS A FOSTER CHILD

With few exceptions, our wild birds here in the United States are satisfactorily faithful in their family affairs. Once mated for the season, male and female are hardly likely to go philandering around any more than they would let their nestlings suffer from hunger. Almost alone among the seven hundred or more different kinds which comprise our feathered population, cowbirds, on the other hand, pay no attention to that good old admonition to "keep thee only unto her"—or him, as the case may be. For such small birds, their lack of moral character is astonishing.

Cowbirds belong to the blackbird tribe and are commonly distributed over almost the entire country; while not actually non-migratory, their seasonal movements north and south are only moderate shifts, so it is not unusual to find some individuals wintering even in New England.

They never mate, in the usual meaning of the term, and during the breeding season the males will pick up with any interested females they meet, and vice versa. The lady carries her irresponsible traits so far that she doesn't even build a home of her own, but goes sneaking around laying her eggs in smaller birds' nests, thus foisting all the incubation and baby-sitting on foster parents.

All this is reprehensible enough, but only the beginning of the trouble, for a cowbird egg hatches very quickly and the young bird grows so fast that it hogs most of the food brought by the substitute parents, so that the legitimate inmates of the nest often starve to death. Usually only a single egg is laid in any one nest, so the total of a dozen or so which one cowbird produces in a season can break

up quite a number of otherwise happy bird homes. As many as
ninety different species are known to be victimized in this way.

You might think that the strangers on which the cowbird saddles
all her maternal problems would either destroy the alien egg before
it hatches or else throw the young interloper out on its ear as soon as
they see its outsize, loutish figure, but for some obscure reason they
seldom do.

Like the gangster movie thriller, cowbird life provides a touch of
comic relief when a male sets out to impress his casual female ac-
quaintances—often several of them—with what a fine, handsome lad
he is. At such times he puffs out his neck, strikes grotesque attitudes,
some of which look as if he were about to be violently seasick, and
accompanies the whole procedure with low-pitched gurgling notes
that sound a bit like water dripping from a faucet into a bowl.

In Nature's scheme even the most unpleasant characters have their
good points. So cowbirds possess the asset of destroying great numbers of insects, many of them noxious, which constitute a large part
of their diet. Here lies the origin of their common name, for you
often see them close to the feet of grazing cattle, or even perched on
their backs, busily hunting the various bugs which pester the animals
or are stirred up from the grass by their movements.

ℐELLOW-BREASTED 𝒞HAT

LARGEST OF OUR WARBLERS

Technically, chats belong to the wood warbler clan, but you'd never suspect it as you hear and occasionally see them in the brushy, tangled fields and lowlands that are their favorite haunts after they come north in the spring from Central America and spread across the country from the Atlantic to the Great Plains and the Northern Tier to the Gulf Coast. True, the males are bright yellow and white below and olive green above—true warbler colors. But there the obvious resemblance ends, and the rest is—well, let's see:

From end to end and inside to out, chats are downright individualists, not to say eccentrics. From the concealment of the tangled cover through which they flit by fits and starts, the springtime males all but shout an astounding medley of mews, clucks, whistles, and barks unmatched by any other species except perhaps the mockingbird. Only after the coarse, catbird-like nests are built and the females have laid their four or five whitish, dark-blotched eggs do the males replace the fantastic extremes of their songs with bursts of richer, more musical notes which seem literally to carry the singers fluttering and gyrating up into the air for all to see. In chat country, at this season, hardly an hour of the day passes without your hearing at least one male expressing himself to the world, even at a quarter-mile distance. Nor is that expression limited to the daylight hours, for frequently it breaks out at intervals during the night, particularly in clear weather.

After the young are out of the nest you rarely hear a word from the chats, except perhaps a low, scolding note from the depths of a thicket. From voluble clowns they change abruptly to silent skulkers, and you might think that they had left the neighborhood completely. But they're still there, reaping their regular harvest of insects and, to a greater extent than other warblers, wild berries and various small fruits. By late August most of them are heading south again, for just as they are among the earlier arrivals in the spring migration, so are they one of the first species to reverse their journey when autumn is just around the corner.

BLACK-CAPPED CHICKADEE

WEE FIGURE, MIGHTY HEART

If chickadees spoke English, it would be easy to imagine one of them calling to its gang through the gloom of a winter blizzard or sleet storm, "Are we downhearted?" and all the other chickadees calling back in chorus, "NO!" For if ever there was a tiny bundle of black, gray, and white feathered energy and optimism, the chickadee is it.

You just can't discourage one of these little tads. Regardless of temperature, weather, or place, it always finds food to keep its engines supplied with fuel—insect eggs and larvae among the tree branches, birch and hemlock seeds, suet and sunflower seeds and peanut butter at feeding stations maintained by people who value the chickadee as the most engaging winter guest a bird lover could ask for. It is the perfect gymnast, hanging upside down from a wind-tossed twig as easily as it clings to the rugged bark of an oak trunk, twitching away at a hibernating beetle. It becomes astonishingly tame where you provide it with winter food, even learning to take a tempting scrap from your fingers if you are quiet and patient. And it always has a lot to say for itself in a saucy, amusing, little-bird sort of way.

Toward the end of the winter you hear with increasing frequency a chickadee call that is incredibly different from the more usual half-scolding *dee-dee-dee-dee* or *chick-a-dee-dee*. It is a fine, high, beautifully clear whistle—*phee-be*—the second note one or two tones lower than the first. This echoes an instinctive feeling that spring is coming and that it will soon be time to find a wife and a suitable punky dead tree stub in which to peck out a roomy, pear-shaped home to house the two of them and a family of sometimes eight or ten little fellow acrobats. By April the small flocks which have roved the woods and orchards and lawn trees all winter break up, and their members become more shy and quiet as they retire to their chosen breeding haunts.

As befits birds of such seeming intelligence and character, chickadee husbands are co-operative and useful around the house. They help in building the family home, share the task of sitting on the eggs, join willingly in the incessant further project of keeping the youngsters' stomachs supplied with food. Also, if occasion arises, they will do their small mightiest to drive away an intruder. It is not known, though, whether they practice a trick ascribed to the mother bird, by the late John Burroughs, when she tires of being too persistently observed while incubating her eggs. The bird, Mr. Burroughs said, apparently draws in its breath until its form perceptibly swells and then expels it with a quick explosive sound like an escaping jet of steam.

Black-capped chickadees migrate but little in the usual sense of the word, and you can find them at all seasons of the year in the Middle, North Central, Middle Atlantic and New England States. North, south, and west of this great area their place is taken by closely allied species which, though they differ slightly in appearance, maintain the true chickadee character and manners.

*R*OSE-BREASTED *G*ROSBEAK

AS GAY IN COLOR AS IN SONG

The sterner sex of this heavy-billed, somewhat less than catbird-size relative of the cardinal comes close to being the perfect American bird. Strikingly garbed in black and white, with a showy shield of bright rose red on his breast and a splash of the same color on the under side of each wing, he is a picture of devil-may-care gallantry, yet no bird is more devoted and helpful to his wife and family. As a singer he ranks with the best, and though originally he lived only in the deep forests, today he is completely at home among the shade trees of suburban towns and villages and really seems to enjoy his contact with mankind. From spring until autumn you are likely to see him in any suitable locality east of the Great Plains and from Canada to the lower Middle West and the Middle Atlantic States. But he doesn't like cold weather and each winter travels to Central America, Colombia, and Venezuela to escape it.

The song of the male rose-breasted is not unlike the robin's as far as the notes are concerned, but the tones are far purer and of greater richness. There is an infectious vim in it, too, as though the bird simply couldn't control his high spirits and happiness. Actually, he is so fond of singing that he often carols to himself while taking his turn at sitting on his mate's four or five eggs in their loose twig and grass nest hidden in a tall shrub or tree—a sharing of family duties to which he seems to have no objection. He is something of a ventriloquist, too, when he happens to think of it. As final evidence of husbandly devotion, he often brings food to the female when she is incubating and is never far away from her.

You might expect such heavy-billed birds to be primarily seed-eaters, but careful checks have shown that rose-breasteds eat about equal quantities of vegetal and insect food. To give you a more definite idea of their broad tastes, they consume numbers of wood borers, leaf beetles, click beetles, scale insects, aphids, curculio beetles, stinkbugs, tent caterpillars, gipsy-moth caterpillars, and Colorado potato beetles. On the plant side, favorite dishes are weed and tree seeds, various wild fruits, many buds, and sometimes cultivated peas. The last item, which is by no means a regular habit, is about the only black mark that we humans can record against a bird that is as beneficial as it is pleasant to have around the place.

115

GREAT BLUE HERON

SENTINEL OF THE WATERSIDE

Throughout the vast area from the Atlantic to the Pacific and Canada to the Gulf of Mexico, any time between early spring and the edge of winter, you may see this big slate-gray "crane" standing sentinel-like in shallow water at the margin of a pond or sluggish river. It is one of our largest American birds, with a standing height that may approach five feet and a wingspread of six. Try to approach it, and you will find that it ranks among the wariest, too, for while you are still several hundred yards away the huge bird is likely to take off on ponderous wings, long neck doubled S-like close to its shoulders, stilt legs trailing out behind.

The great blue is a solitary sort of bird, except during migration and when several or many pairs gather to build their massive stick nests high among the branches of secluded large trees as spring begins to get under way. Though their primary food is fish, frogs, salamanders, meadow mice, and other creatures found only in or near water, the nesting rookery may be many miles from the nearest creek or lake, necessitating much flying to and fro, especially after the three or four pale blue eggs have hatched.

The feeding habits of this picturesque giant are as odd as they are efficient. The technique is to stand motionless for minutes at a time waiting for an unsuspecting fish or frog to come within reach, or else to wade very deliberately through the shallow water until a victim is located. In either case the actual capture takes the same pattern: the long, supple neck darts out from its S-shape posture, driving the six-inch spear bill straight to the mark. So swift is the stroke that your eye cannot follow it, and very rarely does it miss the victim. There's

real power in it, too—plenty to do serious damage to anyone rash enough to get within striking distance of a wounded great blue. There is probably no exaggeration in the report that an angry bird has driven its beak so far through the blade of a pine oar that its tip projected a couple of inches on the far side. Small wonder that great blues have been known to catch and eat fish weighing well over a pound.

The young are fed by regurgitation, a rather murderous-looking operation since it involves the old bird's jabbing its bill far down into its offspring's throat. The kiddies seem to like it, though, for long before they can fly they will leave the nest and clamber out among the branches to meet an incoming parent halfway. Bills, feet, and wings are all used in this acrobatic stunt, but even so a youngster sometimes falls to the ground far below and perishes miserably.

Some of these herons spend the winter as far north as middle New England, but the majority migrate farther south, sometimes even as far as Panama and Venezuela.

$\mathcal{S}$PARROW $\mathcal{H}$AWK

THE PRETTIEST OF ALL THE FALCONS

Actually it is an insult as well as a misnomer to call this pretty little falcon a "sparrow" hawk, for only occasionally does it catch anything with feathers on it. By far the majority of its food consists of mice and spiders, grasshoppers and other insects, so it stands high on the list of beneficial birds. As a matter of fact, so do most of the other hawks, popular belief to the contrary notwithstanding.

Not only is this the smallest American member of the hawk tribe; it is also the most gaily dressed. Slaty-blue wings; bright red-brown back and tail, the latter tipped with black and white; slate blue, black, red-brown, buff, and white for a head pattern; legs yellow and under parts buffy spotted with black—these are the colors of a mature male in full plumage, and his wife is only slightly less dressy. And speaking of the woman in the case, all lady hawks are larger than the menfolks, an odd fact which may or may not have some bearing on their more sober colors.

Sparrow hawks seem to carry a good deal of their vigorous color spirit into their daily business of hunting for food over a vast territory—all of the United States and southern Canada during the warmer months, and in winter through the Middle States and southward as far as Costa Rica. You are most likely to see them in open country, perched erectly on a telegraph pole, electric cable line, or high in a dead tree from which they can get a broad outlook over fields, pasture land, and similar foraging territory. Frighten them, and they will take off with swift, buoyant, almost swallow-like flight, often uttering the high-pitched *killy-killy-killy-killy* which is their characteristic call. But if you are patient and wait quietly at a discreet distance, you may see one actually catching its quarry, one of the most interesting sights in birddom.

A sparrow hawk hunts by sight, perhaps aided at times by its sense of hearing. So, scanning the ground from a high perch, it finally spots a mouse or grasshopper moving in the grass and swoops silently down and away to a point directly over it. There, sometimes thirty or forty feet above the ground, it hovers in one spot, waiting for a favorable moment to drop lightly, claws outstretched. More often than not that swift descent is successful, and the bird wings back to its perch for a leisurely meal.

Other hawks build their nests in the open air, but sparrow hawks express themselves by setting up housekeeping in a tree cavity, often one made originally by a large woodpecker such as the flicker. Here, in spring, the pair may raise as many as six or seven youngsters, and the excited *killy-killying* when the kids finally take to wing is worth going a long way to hear.

GANNET

CHIEF OF THE OCEAN DIVERS

The bird world's grand championship in high diving and underwater swimming undoubtedly belongs to this three-foot feathered thunderbolt with a six-foot spread of wing, the most spectacular flier of the whole North Atlantic. Pure white from bill to tail, save for a yellowish overcast on head, neck, and lower back and stylish black

wing tips, it is a sea-food specialist that catches its own by daring power and speed.

A gannet plunges on its prospective meal from a height of a few yards to sixty or even a hundred feet, depending largely on how deep the fish are swimming. With nearly folded wings the great, powerful bird dives headfirst with amazing speed, closing its wings completely an instant before it hits the water with such velocity that the spray jets upward like a fountain. The deeper the fish the higher the dive, for the impetus must be enough to carry the bird well under water. No doubt the webbed feet come into full play once the hunter is below the surface, and the chances are that the wings, too, are used for propulsion there. At all events, gannets can and do catch a good deal of their prey by outswimming it, often at surprising depths. There are reliable reports of birds becoming caught in fishermen's nets set ninety feet under water.

The gannet is essentially a bird of the North Atlantic, breeding on rocky cliffs in the Gulf of St. Lawrence region, Labrador, Greenland, and among the British Isles. It is a famous colony nester, as you will see if you treat yourself to a trip to Bonaventure Island just off the tip of the Gaspé Peninsula, where some twenty thousand pairs raise their young every summer. Every ledge on the precipitous rock face of the island facing the open ocean is white with them, and the air is full of swooping, soaring, diving forms as the old birds incessantly come and go. Each pair has but a single egg, which takes five or six weeks to hatch. But nesting begins in May and continues until well into July, so that the big show at Bonaventure runs for months.

When their young are on the wing the gannets start moving south, usually keeping well offshore so that your only glimpse of them from land is likely to be just a flash of white in the sky far out at sea. I have seen considerable numbers of them around the mouth of Chesapeake Bay in late November, from the ferry that plies between Norfolk and Cape Charles. A week later the vanguard had reached St. Augustine, Florida, where our binoculars picked them up three or four miles off the beach. That is nearly as far south as most of them go for the winter, for these hardy fishermen have no need, and probably little liking, for balmy weather and a lazy life.

DRE

$\mathscr{B}$ROWN $\mathscr{C}$REEPER

LIKE A FALLING AUTUMN LEAF

Many of our American bird names are based on some visible or audible characteristic. Catbird, for instance, because of one of its calls; or flycatcher, or hummingbird. But you would look far to find a more obvious example of this fact than is furnished by the brown creeper, for if any bird creeps by nature, and looks brown as you see it in the winter woods, this is the one.

Brown creeper is an unobtrusive little lad, rather slender, scarcely over five inches in length from the tip of its slim, curved bill to the end of a rather long, stiffish-pointed tail which serves as a useful prop while spiraling up the rough bark of trees in search of insect-egg or larva meals. The bird doesn't say much, either—merely an occasional faint lisp, perhaps a timid sort of trill, and, by way of a song, five or six thin, high, long-and-short notes with a trace of hiss in them. But it is as busy a scrap of a bird as you are likely to find anywhere in the woods or, especially in fall or winter, among the lawn trees near your house.

Among the brown creeper's most interesting traits is its method of feeding. When you first glimpse a creeper, it may be on the trunk of a good-sized tree, perhaps only a foot from the ground, and astonishingly inconspicuous because of the protective coloring. Almost certainly, though, it will be moving upward in a peculiarly jerky, creeping fashion that carries it along with surprising speed. Now and then it pauses briefly to extract some morsel of food from a bark crevice, then continues the search in more or less of a spiral around the trunk and upward along one of the main branches. Occasionally it may drop down to the base of another limb, but never really retraces its steps. Finally, having reached a point where the smallness of the branch and probably the greater smoothness of the bark make further hunting unprofitable, the creeper looses its hold and, almost like a withered, wind-blown leaf, drops away to the base of another nearby tree and immediately begins a fresh climb.

Although brown creepers often appear among scattered trees during the non-breeding months, their real home is in the forests, especially old ones where the presence of many dead trees provides an abundance of insect food and loose strips of bark under which the creepers like to build their nests of moss, bark shreds, feathers, and sometimes a few twigs. Granted such opportunities, housekeeping for the new family of six or so may be carried on almost anywhere in the vast area from Newfoundland westward to Alaska, into the Border States, and southward along the mountain chains as far as North Carolina and southern California.

The brown creeper belongs to a very small bird family—in fact, it is the only representative in temperate America. But it is not at all embarrassed by loneliness. Often you'll see several creepers tagging along with a flock of chickadees foraging through the woods, perfectly contented, perfectly companionable, entirely self-reliant. Few birds are more likable; none attend more strictly and agreeably to their own business.

$\mathcal{T}$REE $\mathcal{S}$WALLOW

MASTER OF MIGRATION

In late July and August, almost anywhere in the United States north of Georgia, Arkansas, and New Mexico, the tree swallows start gathering into huge flocks which later on will sweep southward even as far as lower Mexico, Guatemala, and Cuba. Nesting time over and the younger generation fully air-borne, parents and offspring alike dart gracefully about the sky or perch by dozens on the telegraph wires, always with their snowy-white breasts facing whatever breeze there may be.

Unlike the barn swallow, tree swallows are cavity nesters—often in hollow trees, as their name suggests, or abandoned woodpecker holes. They and the much larger purple martins are the only ones of their group that will take readily to man-made birdhouses. In one of these, if it is located out in the open, a pair may decide to set up housekeeping as early as the latter part of April, building their nest of grasses and lining it with feathers (chiefly white ones!) as a comfortable bed for three to eight pure-white eggs. The male, apparently, is a good family man, for he shares egg-sitting duties with his mate and, of course, holds up his end of the incessant insect catching required when the time comes to feed the youngsters. In

125

some cases a pair may raise two families in a single season, but one seems to be enough in most cases.

Swallows as a group are insect eaters, but the tree swallow stands apart from all the rest in that it also feeds heavily on the berries of bayberry—the same kind that colonial New Englanders used for making their famous bayberry candles—wherever this hardy bush grows in any abundance. Along the Atlantic Coast, at least, this chilly-weather food supply may be one reason why tree swallows sometimes winter as far north as Connecticut and Massachusetts. And probably, too, it helps to explain why even some individuals which may be going far south often linger in the North until November despite the scarcity of flying insects at that season.

One of the most impressive sights in the American bird world is the vast gatherings of tree swallows in a chosen extensive marsh when summer wanes. At this rendezvous millions gather each afternoon for weeks, settling among the cattails and rushes as darkness nears, rising with the sun to scatter far and wide across the countryside. The manner of their actual southward migration is too imperfectly understood, but some light may be thrown on it by a quotation from the late Dr. Frank M. Chapman's book, *Bird Studies with a Camera.* Writing of one of these vast tree swallow embarkation camps, Dr. Chapman wrote:

"Swallows are not known to migrate by night, and, so far as I am aware, no single swallow has ever been found among the thousands of night-flying birds which have perished by striking lighthouses. The swallows, therefore, when migrating probably leave the marsh during the day, but in what manner who can say?

"Several times when crossing the marshes on the cars I have observed gatherings of swallows which made the immense flocks observed daily in August and September seem little more than a family of birds. They appeared in the distance like a vast swarm of gnats; it was as though all the swallows in the marsh had collected in one great storm of birds. The significance of this movement I have never had the fortune to determine, but it seems highly probable that it is connected with the inauguration of an actual migration toward the birds' winter quarters."

$\mathscr{W}$HOOPING $\mathscr{C}$RANE

LONG OF LEG AND LOUD OF VOICE

This tallest and heaviest of our native wading birds used to be found in substantial numbers over much of North America, but its great size and white plumage made it so conspicuous that, with the added incentive of its fine-flavored meat, hunters pursued it relentlessly, generation after generation. Today we have definite knowledge of only thirty-seven living specimens, and even these owe their existence largely to having been granted a well-guarded federal refuge of over forty thousand acres on the Texas coast where they can pass the winter in comparative safety.

The whooper stands about five feet tall and has a wingspread of nearly eight. It is a bird of open country, such as the prairies and vast fresh-water marshes, where its telescopic vision can detect an enemy at fantastic distances. Here, too, it can find the kinds of food it likes—mice, frogs, lizards, plant roots and seeds, small aquatic creatures, et cetera. Persecution has made it extremely wary, and in the spring, when the few remnants head for their unknown breeding grounds in the Far North, they often fly so high as to be virtually out of sight. How different it must have been in the early nineteenth century when Nuttall, one of the great early ornithologists, said of their migration through the Mississippi Valley, "the clangor of their numerous legions, passing high in air, was almost deafening."

The name "whooping," of course, comes from the character of its call—a loud, ringing challenge which Audubon said he could hear at a distance of three miles when the weather was favorable. The bird also utters various shorter croaks, especially when migrating.

A whooper's nest is a solidly built platform of weeds and rushes, and its site is on land or water in an open marsh or near one. Only two huge eggs are laid, and they have the unusual distinction of being definitely rough on the outside. A single brood a year is the rule, so that the rate of increase cannot but be slow.

What the future of this gigantic bird may hold is an open question, for thirty-seven is a pitifully small number on which to base a substantial comeback. For the present, at least, this little band is holding its own, and perhaps even gaining a trifle. But under the best circumstances it will be years before conservationists will be able to say that they have clearly won their battle to save from extinction one of the most spectacular of America's birds.

LONG-BILLED MARSH WREN

FIVE INCHES OF ENDLESS ENERGY

Tidewater marshes are the places to look for this exuberant atom, and the best time of the year is late spring and early summer. There, if you have chosen the right locality, you will hear constant chatterings and bubbly songs coming from deep in the shelter of the cattails and rushes, punctuated by particularly vehement outbursts as male after male flutters vertically into the air for a few feet and drops back again, as though exploding in an ecstasy of singing. Nowhere

among all the creatures of marsh and swamp will you find a more convincing demonstration of overwhelming enthusiasm and high spirits.

These lovers of the wetlands, only a trifle smaller than the better-known house wrens that patronize your bird boxes so freely, must be born optimists, for in their enthusiasm the males frequently build several more nests than their mates will ever use. More than that, they keep singing while they work, even though their bills may be filled with the cattail fluff which is so freely utilized as lining material. At times the songs are so frequent that all the down is lost before the nest is reached, and the singer has to go back for a fresh supply. Not even darkness puts an end to the music, especially if the moon is out.

Marsh wren nests are quite amazing globes of woven marsh grass, rushes, and so on, sometimes intermixed with mud and attached to cattails, flags, wild rice, or similar growths which hold them safely above the water level. Each has a small entrance hole on one side, and the interior is a singularly soft, snug place for the half-dozen or so brown-spotted eggs. The female does most of the incubating job —not too much of a chore, as hatching usually takes only ten or twelve days. On the other hand, she normally follows the first family with a second and sometimes a third, so altogether she has a pretty busy season.

The nesting range covers the eastern United States and Canada, mostly near the coast, from Virginia to Quebec and New Brunswick, and the winter territory runs from lower Connecticut to South Carolina and Florida. Through much of this area the distribution of the birds is definitely localized, for not every apparently suitable marsh attracts them. Where you do find them, however, there are likely to be a good many pairs, for long-billed marsh wrens are gregarious little beggars and the places they frequent produce enough of their insect food to support a pretty dense population. Along one road which crosses a mile-wide brackish marsh not far from New York City, I have seen a singing male every hundred feet or so, and no doubt there were many more that did not happen to pop upward from the shelter of the cattails while I was passing.

$\mathscr{B}$LACK $\mathscr{S}$KIMMER

NOISY SAILOR WITH PROTRUDING JAW

Why "skimmer"? Well, that's because this big black and white sea bird feeds by flying along so close to the water that, with open mouth, its projecting lower "jaw" skims up the small marine creatures which constitute its diet. Both mandibles are narrow and sharp-edged, a fact which leads to the skimmer's other common names of shearwater, cutwater, and scissorbill.

Skimmers are grotesque-looking characters, with bright red feet and equally brilliant red on the basal halves of their otherwise black bills. They are terrifically noisy when you disturb them on their nesting grounds or on the bars and beaches where they sometimes gather

131

in large flocks. Yaps, screams, and hoarse squawks pour out of them like water from a pitcher, in startling contrast to the consummate grace and beauty of their flight.

The black is the only one of the five members of the skimmer genus that reaches United States water. You will often see it along the shore of the Gulf of Mexico from Texas to Key West, and thence north along the Atlantic Coast as far as Virginia and occasionally Long Island. This area comprises its spring, summer, and autumn range, while in the winter many of the birds move southward to Mexico, Costa Rica, and sometimes the West Indies.

Nest building in May or June is hardly even a formality; the birds merely make slight hollows in the loose sand by squatting down and turning round and round—it's just as simple as that. Normally there are four white to pale buff eggs more or less blotched with darker colors that serve as good camouflage in the barren beach surroundings. The female apparently attends to all the incubation, but her old man frequently stands close by as though to assure her that he isn't off having a good time.

The sand-colored youngsters hatch about twenty-four hours apart, and each is able to run around nimbly when no more than two days old. At this stage their bills are quite normal in appearance, with both mandibles of equal length, so that they can pick up bits of food for themselves to supplement the small fish and other tidbits which their parents bring them from the sea. When you think it over, this makes sense, for there would be no point in having a long lower mandible to "skim" with until there is the power of flight so necessary to the skimming operation.

What with the scuttling around of the dozens or hundreds of young birds, and the cries and gyrations of their parents constantly coming and going, a black skimmer colony at the height of the nesting season is an avian bedlam. Its noisy confusion, though, is nothing as compared to the tumult that breaks loose when a human being approaches. Then the old birds really go into action, screaming at the top of their voices as they swoop straight at the intruder. It looks like a really murderous charge, but the birds veer off just in time, so that one's chance of being actually struck by them is slight.

OBIN

AMERICA'S ALL-TIME FAVORITE

Robins are America's most universal and best-loved birds. Through-out the United States and much of Canada they are true birds of the people, liking the open, friendly country where humans live, raising their two or three broods a year in villages, orchards, farm lands, parks, big estates, and little dooryards. The cheery, full-throated warbling of the males is the universal bird song of May. From early spring to middle autumn a lawn without its complement of robins would hardly be a lawn at all.

Actually, these hearty, reddish-breasted favorites are thrushes, and

133

they build typical thrush nests of twigs, grasses, and various fibrous materials well cemented with mud carried in their beaks from the nearest wet spot. If natural mud cannot be found, the female (she usually does most of the construction while the male stands guard and feeds her occasionally) has been known to fill her bill with dust and then dip it in a birdbath, or even wet her feathers and then shake off the drops in a dusty road.

The nesting sites are as cosmopolitan as the birds that choose them. Tree crotches or branches; nooks on buildings, bridges, wagons, boats; fence posts, stone walls, bushes, porch vines, rose arches, man-made nesting shelves—robins like them all, whether they be a few or seventy feet from the ground. Once incubation of the four or five greenish-blue eggs begins, the female carries on with little or no help from her mate, but he does his full share of food gathering for the young even after they leave the nest.

Male robins stage noisy and spectacular battles with each other during the courtship season, and after the matches have been made and housekeeping begins, each cockbird is constantly on the watch against poaching on his territory by others of his kind whose presence might mean a lessened food supply for his family. Sometimes he carries this solicitude to the extreme of fighting his own reflection in a window or in the polished hubcap of a car, continuing the futile battle for days unless something is done to obliterate the reflecting surface.

While robins are the traditional heralds of spring in the Northern States, the fact is that a good many of them actually spend the winter even in New England, especially if they find thick plantings of cedar or pine trees and a plentiful supply of such foods as the berries of juniper, bayberry, hawthorn, and sumac. Probably these are birds that summered farther north, taking the place of New Englanders that had moved southward themselves, for the species is definitely migratory. You see clear evidence of this characteristic in the sizable flocks which appear in the fall, virtually vanish, and reappear in the spring. During the winter months vast assemblages establish roosting places in parts of the South; one such haunt in North Carolina was estimated to contain three million birds.

HERRING GULL

NATURE'S SANITARY DEPARTMENT

This is the omnipresent gull of Atlantic coastal waters from Florida
to the Arctic, the same big fellow which, as an adult, is largely pearl
gray above and white beneath, or dusky brownish in the case of
younger birds. You will also find it on the Great Lakes and, if you
travel that far, on our West Coast from Alaska to Lower California,
from Greenland to northern France, the Baltic, and on the Mediter-
ranean and Caspian seas. Quite a bird and quite a range!

Perhaps it is the herring gull's willingness to eat just about any kind of food anywhere that enables it to succeed over so many miles whose climate ranges from tropical to polar. Thousands of the birds congregate in winter on the garbage dumps of the larger coastal cities, patrol their harbors, and perch on their water-front piers and buildings. Others follow the coastwise ships, looking for anything edible that the cooks or passengers throw overboard. You might, indeed, call them the prize scavengers of the coast, as uncritical of their diet as the vultures are on land.

The "herring" part of the name, of course, comes from the birds' ability to catch small fish that swim near the surface of the water. They are adept, too, at robbing mergansers and other diving ducks of the food that they bring up from greater depths, and have learned a unique technique of their own for mastering the stout shells of the clams that they pick up at low tide along the beaches. When it finds one of these tidbits the gull carries it in its bill thirty or forty feet into the air, drops it on the hard sand or rocks to crack the shell, and follows closely to gobble the meat inside. Since a concrete road makes a better shell-breaker, the gulls will use that if near at hand, and it is not at all unusual to find such a highway littered with fragments of clam armor.

The principal American breeding areas of these resourceful and masterly fliers are the coastal islands of Maine and similar islands in large fresh-water lakes such as Champlain and the Great Lakes. Here they breed in colonies that may contain thousands of birds, each pair building a nest of seaweeds, eelgrass, or general litter directly on the ground or rocks, as the case may be. There is only one brood a year, consisting of three or four youngsters, but as these start wandering around on foot long before they are able to fly, complications are frequent when it comes to feeding them by the customary regurgitation process. Apparently the parents are able to recognize their own offspring, but not vice versa. Consequently, since young herring gulls are always hungry, they frequently try to beg food from a parent not their own and get well beaten up for their impertinence. Sometimes this punishment is so severe that the youngster is killed, though probably by accident rather than design in most instances.

$\mathscr{S}$HRIKES

THEY HANG THEIR FOOD ON NATURE'S HOOKS

Shrikes are deceptive characters. Superficially they look like innocent gray and white songbirds with black masks across their eyes, about the size of robins and occasionally singing rather in the fashion of a mockingbird or brown thrasher, though with less volume and richness. You would never guess, unless their powerful hooked beaks made you suspicious, that actually they are ruthless killers that often seem to slay just for the grim joy of it. Furthermore, when one of them has caught and killed a smaller bird, mouse, or large insect like a grasshopper, he often hangs it on a spine of a thorny tree or bush, a barbed-wire fence, or in the fork of a branch, much as an old-time butcher suspends a leg of lamb from a hook in his shop. Small wonder that many people call him butcher-bird.

137

There are two American species of this misleading bird tribe: the northern shrike, breeding from the limit of trees southward to lower Ontario and Quebec and wintering irregularly as far south as Virginia and Kentucky; and the loggerhead, which breeds from Florida northward to the lower edge of its relatives' nesting range. They resemble each other quite closely in appearance as well as in habits, but the loggerhead seems to be more insectivorous than the northern, perhaps because, on the whole, it spends more time in regions which are not blanketed with snow and therefore are more productive of available insect food.

You are most likely to see a shrike perched on some high lookout point, such as a bare treetop or telegraph wire. It is almost invariably alone, a heavy-headed, short-necked bird holding its tail a little higher than the line of the body but occasionally tilting it as if saluting.

From this observation post a shrike's keen eyes can detect the least movement of potential prey in the bushes or grasslands below. When the right moment comes the shrike will probably do one of two things: plunge straight at the victim with surprising speed or, if circumstances are different, hover directly over the quarry before dropping on it like a plummet. In either event the strike is almost always successful, and the butcher-bird kills the victim by a few sharp blows on the head before carrying it away in feet or bill (sometimes both) to a chosen spot where it can be hung up and eaten piece by piece or, perhaps, left dangling for a future meal.

A third method of capture is applied particularly when the quarry is a bird—sparrow, chickadee, or what have you. Here it is a case of straight speed flying plus uncanny ability to follow every twist and turn of the terrified victim. More often than not the shrike is master of the situation, and it can even catch such fast movers as the imported starling.

Both kinds of shrikes build substantial, bulky nests of twigs, leaves, and so on, generally only a few yards above the ground in a thorny bush or dense tree. The number of their pale eggs with darker markings ranges from four to seven, and occasionally two broods are raised in a single season.

$\mathcal{F}$OX $\mathcal{S}$PARROW

RUNNER-UP IN THE FAMILY BEAUTY SHOW

One good look at this large economy-size sparrow and you know where it gets its name, for the upper side of the tail is bright rufous-red and there is a strong tinge of this same foxy color on back and wings. The bird is fox-like in more than color, too, for no other member of the sparrow tribe can equal it in scratching away the dead leaves, and even snow, in busy search for seed or insect food. Foxy really makes things fly, hopping from the ground and, while still in the air, kicking the obstruction backward with both feet.

Fox sparrows are birds of the wild, with much of the free spirit of the Far North in their habits and make-up. In October and November, when they pass through the northern tier of states on the way from their Canadian breeding grounds to their winter range in the Middle States and southward to Florida and the Gulf, you are much more likely to find them in the woods and secluded thickets than around human habitations. Sometimes the first indication of their presence is the rustle of their scratching among the bushes as you walk along an unfrequented country road on a still day. Again, they may disclose their presence by a loud *smack* note of alarm, or a short *chip* which, once heard and identified, you are not likely to forget. Only in early spring, when they reappear on the way northward, is there much chance that you will hear the short but rich and unsparrow-like fluting which is their song.

Of our true sparrows, with the possible exception of the white-crowned, the fox is definitely the most handsome. It always seems a little out of place when it comes south, perhaps because of a certain ruggedness in looks and manners by comparison with other members of the family. It is easy to imagine him and his mate, in the wilderness of Labrador or Saskatchewan or Alaska, building their large, sturdy nest of moss, dry grasses, and leaves and lining it warmly with hair or feathers against the chill of the northern spring. Snow may still be on the ground when they begin, forcing them to choose a spot a few feet up in a tree or bush. But if the earth itself is bare, that is the preferred location.

Not too much is known of the fox sparrow's family life while in the North. It is thought, though, that the female takes over most if not all of the incubation of the four or five pale greenish eggs with their heavy brownish markings, and that it takes about two weeks for them to hatch. Occasionally a pair may raise a second brood, if they start the first one in early June, but the warm season is brief in the North Country, and the chances are that a single family is as much as can usually be managed.

$\mathcal{E}$LF $\mathcal{O}$WL

COMICAL COUNTERPART OF SNOW WHITE'S DWARFS

We give you now the tiniest of all the owls, no longer than an English sparrow. A round-eyed, solemn, grayish-brown mite with white "eyebrows," so comical in appearance that you might take it for a relative of Snow White's seven dwarfs. All day it hides in a hole in a giant cactus trunk, waiting for darkness to come so it will feel safe to flit about over the desert catching ants, grasshoppers, and beetles

and excitedly chattering *chew-chew-chew-chew* or *whi-whi-whi-whi-whi* as earnestly as any orator.

There are many of these funny little characters in the desert country of the Southwest and on into southeastern California, but you would never suspect their presence unless you know the wild life of the region intimately. About the only real "trees" in that land are the saguaro cacti, whose thick spires, sometimes forty feet tall, provide ample diameter for woodpeckers to hollow out their traditional nesting cavities in them. Some of the larger plants have several of these retreats which, after their makers have abandoned them, make perfect homes for the little owls. There, hidden from sight and protected from even the infrequent storms, the elf females lay their two to five pure-white eggs and, in due course, bring forth a new generation of dwarfs to carry on the family tradition.

Actually, these nesting cavities are far more enduring than comparable ones made in trees of woody character, for when a hole has been cut in a living saguaro the plant immediately starts to form scar tissue over the surface of the wound to protect itself from bleeding to death. Thus what began as a simple woodpecker cavity becomes an all but indestructible receptacle that will last as long as the tree itself. Each year the woodpeckers cut fresh holes for themselves, so there are always plenty of accommodations for the owls.

Several other species of birds, including flycatchers, martins, and sparrow hawks, utilize these abandoned woodpecker cavities through the years. A saguaro may live for a century, and I like to think of the possibility that a young pair of elf owls may sometimes move into a veteran home where an ancestor of one of them was hatched twenty or thirty bird generations ago. What a story that would be to tell the youngsters, if owls knew and did such things. And what tales of its varied tenants the old saguaro must know, too, if it could only put them into words!

WHIP-POOR-WILL

THE BIRD WITH THE NON-STOP VOICE

Whip-poor-wills have been characterized as animated insect traps, which is probably as concise a way as any to describe not only the nature of their food but also their method of capturing it by flying about at night and engulfing large moths and small bugs alike in their cavernous mouths. To most people, though, a whip-poor-will is simply a mysterious voice somewhere out in the country darkness—mysterious and astoundingly, incredibly, impossibly repetitious. Any bird that can say *whip-poor-will* two hundred or more times in quick succession without a noticeable pause for breath, and always in clear, ringing tones that are audible a quarter mile away, is entitled to be called amazing solely on that score. But the plain truth is that this is only one of this fantastic bird's oddities.

Whip-poor-wills reach the Middle States in late April from their wintering range in the Deep South and Central America, and within a few weeks have spread all the way from North Carolina and Kansas to lower Canada and from the Atlantic westward to the Plains. Your first notice that they are back will probably be the sound of the males' vigorous "whipping" calls from the dark woods and brushy lowlands. Perhaps, if you are lucky, you may glimpse one swooping bat-like and noiselessly through the dusk or, by day, fluttering up from almost underfoot and dropping back to earth a short distance away as you walk through its haunts. Almost never will you get a good view of the bird unless you have the eyes of an Indian or an owl, for the coloration of a whip-poor-will matches the woodland floor so perfectly that only by accident could you tell crouching bird from fallen leaves.

Whip-poor-wills build no nests—merely lay their two white, blotched eggs right on the ground and trust to the perfect camouflage of the brooding female's plumage to keep them out of danger. Actually, the parents seem to put much more thought and effort into the courtship that precedes the nesting, which is described as an amusingly human sort of love affair replete with a variety of low, confidential clucks and *gaw-gaws* and much bowing and sidling back and forth.

Once the young are hatched they are raised right in the nest, unless too much disturbance occurs, in which case the mother bird flutters around the intruder with guttural cries or tumbles along the ground pretending that she is hurt, hoping to lead the enemy away from the nest.

*R*UFFED *G*ROUSE

KING OF AMERICAN GAME BIRDS

If the tarpon is worthy of the title "silver king" bestowed on him by fishermen, then certainly the ruffed grouse of our Northern States and Canada deserves the description "king of American game birds." Rugged, swift of flight, endlessly resourceful, more beautifully patterned than the rarest weavings of the Far East, it has personality plus and character to spare. Not in all our native bird population will you find a finer example of royal bearing, self-reliance, and good looks.

This striking fellow is primarily a lover of the forested hill country where human beings are few and freedom of range unlimited.

143

Here, in spring, the male can walk stealthily to a favorite stump or fallen tree trunk and, mounting it, look and listen undisturbed before standing erect and, with black neck ruffs raised and tail spread, beating out the notes which serve him as mating song. This is one of the most distinctive sounds of the woods, audible a half mile away on still days—a series of muffled thumps, the first few slow and measured, the rest accelerating smoothly into a drum roll that slows somewhat just before the end. Opinions differ as to how the sound is produced, but the probability is that each thump is a separate power blow on the air with both wings; often, when frightened into flight, the grouse whirs away with a somewhat similar noise.

After mating, the female slips away to undertake alone the task of incubating her eight, twelve, or more whitish eggs and caring for the chicks that hatch from them. Her nest is no more than a depression in the dead leaves of the woodland floor, often at the base of a tree trunk or boulder. It may be quite unconcealed save by the perfect protective coloration of the old bird as she sits motionless on her eggs; often, when she goes on a brief excursion for food, she covers them with leaves to escape the attention of a prowling fox or other marauder.

The young birds, which look for all the world like miniature brown baby chicks, can run almost as soon as they hatch, and the mother bird takes full charge of them until after they have learned to fly well. She is a model parent, teaching them to find food, brooding them under her fluffed feathers at night or on rainy days, battling a potential enemy or leading him away by pretending to have a broken wing. She is a strict disciplinarian, too, and the youngsters instantly obey her varied admonitions to scatter, hide, come to her or be at ease, as she deems best. One of the pleasantest of all bird sights is a hen grouse cautiously crossing a wood road with her mouse-size family following her like wee mechanical toys.

Strangest of all, perhaps, are the "snowshoes" which the ruffed grouse grows in autumn to keep from sinking too deeply into the winter snow. Each toe, then, becomes fringed with flexible horny points which, spreading under the bird's weight, provide much-needed support.

$\mathcal{R}$ED $\mathcal{C}$ROSSBILL

A LAW UNTO ITSELF

At this time we wish to introduce to you, ladies and gentlemen, one of the world's most erratic birds. Perhaps the red crossbill has its own good reasons for roaming around the country without regard for season or weather, but to us it seems to be just plain irresponsible. You may find it in Quebec in the winter and in the Georgia mountains in the summer, or vice versa. A crossbill pair may start building their substantial twig, grass, and moss nest in January, or not until July; usually it will contain four or five eggs and be located in a fir tree, but sometimes they place it out on a bare, leafless limb. While their principal range is in the great coniferous forests north of our Canadian border, they sometimes wander far southward of that area and do not return for a year. Their attitude toward migration seems to be that they can either take it or leave it alone.

The full reasons for such odd behavior are obscure, but it is generally accepted that variations in regional food supply account for a good deal of the strange wandering. A shortage of coniferous tree seeds in the Far North, for example, probably accounts for the occasional southward movement of such large numbers into the New England and Middle States that bird-watchers in these areas enthusiastically proclaim it "a crossbill winter." Another theory is that exceptionally heavy and long-lasting snow cuts off the supply of grit which they need as a digestion aid and thus forces an exodus. Some authorities even weigh the possibility that local food supply variations have a bearing on the irregularity of the nesting season.

Like most birds essentially accustomed to wilderness forests, crossbills are so unsuspicious of mankind that often you can approach within a few yards before they fly away, especially if they are feeding

on evergreen cones. At such times the reason for the curiously crossed tips of their beaks is clearly demonstrated, for they are perfectly adapted to wrenching off the cone scales to expose the seeds, which are then picked out with the tongue. This is highly specialized equipment, of course, and is something of a handicap when the birds eat other foods—elm seeds, for instance, or beechnuts, or sometimes caterpillars. But the crossbills get around it somehow, even if they have to turn their heads sideways to pick up something from the ground.

Both the red crossbill and its close relative, the white-winged, immediately suggest sparrow-sized parrots when you see them clambering deliberately about in the branches of a pine, spruce, or hemlock. They take hold with their bills almost as much as with their feet, and readily hang by one foot while they reach out with the other for a different grip. It is even said, on reliable authority, that when a crossbill is suddenly frightened, it may swing head downward and hang there motionless, perhaps in the hope that its shape, size, and general dull red and brown color will fool the enemy into thinking that it's only an old cone, after all.

$\mathcal{Y}$ELLOW-SHAFTED $\mathcal{F}$LICKER

JOLLY GENTLEMAN OF HOME AND ORCHARD

Flickers are by all odds the largest of our common woodpeckers, and in some ways are so different from the rest of their family that at times you wonder if they don't belong to some other race. For one thing, they are predominantly brownish and black rather than blackish and white, and for another, their bills are sharp-pointed and a little curved instead of straight and chisel-like. Finally, they spend much of their time on the ground hunting for ants, and while there they run and stop almost as agilely as a robin.

Of course they do have many regular woodpecker traits, such as chopping big nesting holes in dead trees, drumming loudly on resonant limbs, and propping themselves with stiff-pointed tail feathers while they climb up tree trunks searching for insect grubs under the bark. They are cheerful and noisy souls, too, saying a surprising number of bird words in loud but rather pleasing tones and making a great display of their really lovely plumage during the spring courting season.

Such a big, showy bird is bound to attract widespread attention, so it is not surprising that the flicker is credited with having more than a hundred common names, most of them arising from some prominent characteristic. Thus, "high-hole" comes from its nest location; "flicker," "wake-up," and "harrywicket" stem from characteristic call notes; and "yellow-hammer" and "golden-winged wood-pecker" result from the bright yellow under sides of wings and tail.

These handsome, jovial extroverts are found in fairly open country all the way from the Gulf Coast to Labrador and west to the Rockies, and while most of those in the North move somewhat southward in autumn, through most of the range you are likely to see at least an occasional bird even in midwinter. They breed throughout this whole vast territory, the males and females sharing the job of chiseling out a pear-shaped hole about a foot or so deep, with a three-inch entrance hole at the top. If they find a promising natural cavity they may use that too, and a naturalistic birdhouse of the right dimensions sometimes attracts them also. The nest may be anywhere from five to ninety feet from the ground, and if suitable trees are scarce, the birds often hack out homes in telegraph poles or large fence posts.

Flickers have no use for race suicide, and though they usually have only one brood a year, it is likely to be a big one. Both parents share the task of hatching the five to ten or more pure-white eggs, and when the young are on the wing the whole family often turns to a fruit diet, especially of wild cherries, pepperidge berries, and even bayberry and poison ivy.

$\mathcal{B}$ARN $\mathcal{S}$WALLOW

THE LAST WORD IN AIR-BORNE GRACE

Mastery of the air is achieved by many kinds of birds, but none combines it with more perfect grace than the barn swallow, one of our commonest and most popular species. Skimming low over the mown hayfield, darting across the blue of a summer sky in pursuit of insects lured to high flight by the pleasant weather, sweeping nonchalantly through an open window or doorway into the dim recesses of a barn where its mud-daubed nest is plastered to a rafter, this swallow never misses a wingbeat nor makes an awkward movement.

For all their daring skill on the wing, barn swallows are friendly birds, twittering sociably among themselves and quickly becoming accustomed to the presence of people within a few feet of their nests. Sometimes several pairs will raise their families amicably in the same old barn, and frequently you will find them building in a small garage or along the eaves of a suburban railroad station, completely unworried by the noises and bustling of mankind. Usually there are two broods a season, sometimes three, and each clutch consists of four or five white eggs nestled snugly in the soft grass and feather lining of the nest. Oddly enough, the young of the first brood sometimes help their parents feed the second lot, an almost unprecedented occurrence among birds.

These versatile little birds have a tremendous range, wintering from Florida and southern California to Brazil, Argentina, and Chile, and coming north in early spring to spread over most of North America as far up as Alaska, central Quebec, and Newfoundland. They migrate freely by daylight, for their speed and agility in the air give them virtual immunity from sudden death by hawks. The barn swallow's food consists entirely of insects, quite literally captured on the wing. It is the pursuit of this daily bread that accounts for the bird's erratic flight, of course.

This is the swallow which you often see skimming along a millpond or quiet river on a summer's day, dipping occasionally to leave quick-spreading rings on the water's surface. Sometimes these dainty pauses are to snatch up some aquatic insects, sometimes to scoop a wee drink of water. In both cases the purpose is accomplished entirely with the bill and so deftly that not a feather is wet. At other times the birds are bathing, and then they make definite dips into the water before adjourning to a nearby perch to preen and dry themselves in the sunshine.

ROSEATE SPOONBILL

TOO GROTESQUE TO BE BELIEVED

To see one of these long-legged pink and white waders for the first time is to wonder why in the world Mother Nature ever designed so fantastic a bird. It's a big fellow, a little over thirty inches long overall, and the skin of its featherless head and throat is varicolored with orange, black, and dull green. At the base of its neck, in front, a tuft of short pink plumes sets off the otherwise buffy feathers, and out in front of everything else is that amazing six-inch spatulate bill whose shape is the reason for the bird's peculiar name.

Nature does nothing without a good reason, though, and so the spoonbill's "spoon" serves a real and practical purpose. The birds feed on small aquatic creatures of one sort and another, which they catch by wading along while they swing their big, opened bills from side to side through the mud and water—a little like a human being trying to ladle out the letters in a bowl of alphabet soup.

Spoonbills are Southerners, found here and there on the Texas and Louisiana coasts and in southern Florida. They breed in rookeries, building stick platform nests ten feet or so up among the cypresses and mangroves in dense, secluded marshes. Here they lay three or four white, spotted eggs whose contents, when they hatch, soon start to act like the old folks, swinging their heads and necks eagerly when they see a parent approaching with food. There is this difference, though: a grown-up spoonbill is a decidedly silent bird, save for an occasional croak, whereas the kiddies whistle tremulously, and louder and louder, as dinner draws nearer.

In the days of the unrestricted feathers-for-millinery trade spoonbills were so relentlessly pursued by the plume hunters that there was grave danger of their being exterminated. Had it not been for

151

the establishment of suitable sanctuaries, protected by armed guards, it is doubtful if you could see one of these astonishing birds alive today. But apparently their fate is now well around its dangerous corner, and so they should be with us for a long, long time to come.

Louisiana Water-Thrush

VOICING THE SPIRIT OF THE RUSHING STREAMS

The mere mention of this big, shy warbler's name recalls early summer days along the clear, rocky streams of lower New York and New England, where the essence of the woodland and the leaping current seemed caught up and distilled into a wild, ringing song that has no equal in all our native bird repertoire. You seldom see the singer, except as he darts up and down stream with amazing speed. But his voice, free and spirited as the winds and the waterfalls, can never be forgotten.

There are two water-thrushes in the eastern United States—the Louisiana, and the northern. Both are quite similar in appearance, but the former is the finer singer to most human ears. The northern breeds in upper New England and Canada all the way across the country and spends the winter from the Bahamas and southern Florida down through Mexico and Lower California to the Guianas and Colombia. The Louisiana's nesting range, on the other hand, is from middle New England and the Midwest down to the Carolinas, Georgia, Alabama, and Texas. It spends the winter, oddly enough, in the same tropical regions chosen by its cousin.

Louisiana water-thrushes come north quite early in the spring and head southward again by midsummer. They love the wooded water-

side and usually build their marvelously concealed nests almost literally overhanging it. Sometimes they choose a stump cavity as a site, but more often their choice is under an overhanging bank or among the tangled, exposed roots of a tree. Here, with dead leaves, moss, and twigs, they put together a comfortable, often domed hiding place for their five white eggs, lining it with soft grass, rootlets, or hair. Unless you know exactly where it is, you could easily pass by within a yard and never suspect a thing, so perfectly is the secret hidden.

I have often wondered whether the principles of camouflage so well demonstrated by the Louisiana water-thrush's nest may not have a sort of echo in a curious habit constantly practiced by the bird itself. When, as occasionally happens, you see one on the margin of a stream or perched on a branch above it, you cannot fail to notice the way its body constantly tips or tilts up and down with a smoothly undulating grace which immediately suggest the surface of the swift-flowing stream near by. Some other waterside birds have the same trait, notably the spotted sandpiper and the dipper or water ouzel of the Far Northwest. Perhaps this is just an idle speculation with no basis in scientific fact—I don't know. But stranger things than that are known to exist in the amazing panorama of birds.

$\mathscr{M}$AN-O'-WAR $\mathscr{B}$IRD

TROPICAL INDOLENCE IS IN ITS BLOOD

The American Tropics are a lazy land, and when you see a group of man-o'-war birds circling and floating high in the air above the Bahamas, the southern Florida Keys, or westward along the Gulf Coast, apparently without the slightest motion of their amazingly long, slender wings, you cannot escape the notion that the general indolence of the region is in their blood. For the frigate bird, as some call it, seems never in a hurry, never in a worry, but always willing to drift for hours on invisible air currents and watch the sky stay up.

They are odd-looking birds, these sea gliders with their six to seven feet of wingspread and their long, forked tails usually closed

156

so that they form a single point. Their thin bills are hooked at the tip, their feet surprisingly weak, their color a muddy sort of black all over in the case of males, relieved by white chests where females and young are concerned, plus the all-white heads and necks of the latter. Besides, all ages and sexes have distensible throat pouches designed to accommodate the fish they catch themselves or, more frequently, steal from other and more industrious seafaring birds. Here is their one spot of bright color, for when the breeding season arrives in January and February each male pouch shows carmine-red.

Of course these amazing feathered floaters do not spend all their time drifting through space. When the time comes they gather in dense colonies on favorite isolated islands so generously scattered in those parts of the ocean, and build rickety twig nests in the tops of low trees and scrubby sea grapes or other brush. There is only one white egg to a pair, but both parents are admirably devoted to it and divide the incubation job until the completely naked youngster breaks out of the shell. Often several nests are built within reaching distance of each other, but family feuds are few. Maybe they just don't seem worth the effort!

Infant man-o'-wars are no Adonises, even after they have acquired their nestling coats of white down. Like their elders, they are mostly wings, and in time these become so long that they hang down over the edges of the nests as though their owners had neither the strength nor ambition to furl them properly. About the only sound anyone in the family makes is a bit of squealing and bill-snapping by the younger generation when something out of the ordinary happens. The old bird is said to utter an occasional croak, but few people have heard it.

But man-o'-war life is not always such a somnolent affair. Occasionally some of these super-fliers are caught in the swirl of a violent hurricane roaring out of the Tropics and up the Atlantic Coast, and swept northward to New England or even farther. How many of these strays ever make their way back home is a matter of conjecture, but some at least have been found dead after the storm had passed, apparently killed by exhaustion and lack of food.

RUBY-CROWNED KINGLET

THE MIGHTY ATOM OF OUR SONGBIRDS

A midget among birds, a giant in energy, hardihood, and spirit—this might be a tabloid description of the ruby-crowned. In the summer it lives in the evergreen forest of the North, building a neat nest of moss and lichens for a half-dozen or so creamy-white eggs, and sometimes undertaking a second brood. Then, in autumn, it heads southward to spend the winter from the Middle States as far down as Florida, Mexico, and Guatemala. Quite a program for a four-inch mite whose wings, when spread, reach no more than across your opened hand!

On his breeding grounds, and as most of us know him in the northbound spring migration, the male ruby-crowned is a superlative singer. Though his lower larynx, the part of the throat that produces the song, is no bigger than a fair-sized pinhead, it pours out a volume of sound which, were it proportioned to human throats, would enable us to converse easily at a distance of a mile. You are likely to hear it from the depths of the lawn shrubbery or a low, bushy tree—a merry, infectious bubbling of pure, full-throated phrases on a rising scale, defying exact description but so hearty and zestful that you simply cannot believe its author is so tiny. If you should see him at all, it will be but a momentary glimpse of a plump, olive-colored bird with a white eye ring that gives him a ludicrously staring expression. Time after time, though, he will be merely a voice, the most electric, intriguing voice in the whole bright spring day.

Kinglets belong to a subfamily of the Old World warblers. We have only two species here: the ruby-crowned and the golden-crowned, very similar in appearance except that the male of the latter has an orange streak edged with yellow along the middle of his head, while in the ruby-crowned this patch is vermilion-red. Their habits are similar, too, but the golden-crowned spends the winter farther north than its cousin and is a pleasing but much less spectacular singer. Even in Massachusetts and lower Vermont you may find it wintering, especially among spruce or pine woods.

Probably the long, thick, fluffy plumage of both our kinglets is one reason why they can withstand as much cold weather as they do without harm to their tiny, always busy little bodies. And no doubt another is the industry with which they keep their tummies filled with insect eggs, larvae, and other similar food gleaned from cones, twigs, bark, and all manner of hiding places.

$\mathscr{B}$ALD $\mathscr{E}$AGLE

A TYPICAL AMERICAN?

Our national emblem belongs to no political party, of course, but that does not save it from being a perpetual storm center of controversy between those who scorn it as a feathered robber, carrion-eater, general low-liver, and a coward in the face of attack by king-birds smaller than its own head, and equally vociferous folk who see it as the epitome of all that is great and noble. Actually, both factions are partly right, which perhaps goes to show that the big fellow with the white head is just a typical American, after all.

There can be no question about the bald eagle's majesty on the wing, for it is a superbly masterful flier and soarer, with an over-all length of thirty to thirty-seven inches and a wingspread of six to seven and a half feet, depending on sex and age. As with other birds of prey, the females are larger than their mates. Oddly enough, too, during the first year after the two or three young leave the nest they are appreciably larger than their own parents, measuring as much as an extra foot from wing tip to wing tip. Incidentally, these young birds are three or four years old before they acquire the white heads and tails characteristic of the adults.

Bald eagles are primarily fish-eaters, though catching their own alive is not one of their strong points. In the main they rely on dead fish which they find floating in the water or lying on shore, and others which they steal from hard-working ospreys or fish hawks—often after bullying the smaller fishermen rather roughly to make them drop their prey. The eagles also catch wild ducks on occasion, for they are swift fliers and strike with devastating power. Rabbits and other animals up to the size of foxes are fair game for them too. Fantastically keen eyesight enables them to spot food of any nature at unbelievable distances.

These eagles mate for life, and a pair is likely to return to the same nest for many years, gradually increasing its size as they repair

damage suffered during their months of absence. Eventually their family home may become a colossal affair of branches, sticks, and various odds and ends; the largest one thus far recorded measures twenty feet deep and nine and one half feet wide. Among the customary construction materials a nest often contains strange objects, such as a discarded shoe, big shells, or an empty bottle, for the birds seem to have a fancy for collecting novelties. The site is almost always in the top of the biggest, tallest tree in the neighborhood, and generally not far from a large body of water, either salt or fresh.

There are really two forms or "races" of bald eagle—the southern and the northern. The only physical difference is in size, the latter race being somewhat the larger. The breeding range of the southern is from the Gulf Coast and Florida north to the Carolinas; from this area both young and old birds travel much farther north for the summer after nesting is over, returning to their old haunts in autumn. In the case of the northern race, breeding is chiefly restricted to the region between the Arctic, the Great Lakes, and northern New England, with a few nests scattered farther south. The northerners move irregularly southward in winter, the determining factor apparently being the weather and its effect on their food supply. When all water is frozen over, it becomes a case of no more available fish, so the eagles head for a warmer climate.

For many years Florida was a notably favored nesting region for southern bald eagles, but recently a series of misfortunes in the way of severe storms and cold spells coming at critical times has upset their breeding timetable and resulted in curtailment of their numbers. For once, man's depredations seem to have played little part in the decimation, for public interest in the protection of bald eagles has never been as high in Florida as it is now. What the birds face, apparently, is one of Nature's own acts, so often illogical from our human standpoint. Eagles are among our most steadfast birds, with exceptionally strong attachments to their homes and easily upset by misadventures occurring there. Will they eventually recover their poise, and gradually regain their former abundance? Or can that goal be reached before the increasing development of Florida makes suitable nesting sites too few and far between?

$\mathcal{A}$MERICAN $\mathcal{G}$OLDFINCH

NEVER DOWNHEARTED, WHATEVER HAPPENS

To some the goldfinch is "thistle-bird" and to others "wild canary," but to one and all it is just about the most engaging scrap of bird life to be found in a long, long day. To see a male in his black and gold spring finery feeding daintily at a dandelion seed head in the May sunshine is to know one of the high moments of bird-watching. And when, some bleak December day, a flock of these intrepid little fellows in their sober winter plumage darts overhead in swift, dipping flight, you impulsively wish them well wherever they may be bound.

There is excellent justification for calling this small finch a "wild canary," for in both coloring and voice the males strongly suggest

163

our most popular cage bird. So, too, is " thistle-bird" an apt moniker, for the goldfinch loves to feed on ripe thistle seeds, just as it does on those of the sunflower, black birch, hornbeam, and a host of other garden as well as wild plants. Primarily it is a vegetarian and, like the sparrow tribe, consumes prodigious quantities of weed seeds. Occasionally this last predilection gets it into serious trouble, for there are instances of goldfinches becoming caught and held by the strong hooks of ripened burdock heads on which they had been feeding. In spring, of course, seeds are less plentiful, and in consequence the birds turn to insects, which seem to suit them very well.

Most birds start to raise their families in spring, but goldfinches are individualists and don't begin nest-building until July, August, or even September. If birds were more governed by motives like ours, we might guess that this unusual delay resulted from the desire to be happy and carefree through those grand spring and early summer days. But actually the reason may be tied up with the fact that the young are fed largely on semidigested seeds which their parents regurgitate directly into their mouths, and early in the season there just would not be enough seeds to do the job right. If you wonder why sparrows and other roughly comparable species don't do likewise—well, probably Old Mother Nature alone knows the answer to that one.

Goldfinches cheerfully make the best of their opportunities where they find them, and so their tree nests are well-built cups of fine grasses, bark strips, and moss, well lined with thistledown and holding three to six eggs. It has been said, with some justification, that a newly completed nest is so perfectly constructed that it could hold water. Certainly it is a snug, thoroughly favorable place for a small bird to start life, particularly when it is managed by parents who take as good care of their offspring as goldfinches do.

In spring, summer, and early fall you are likely to see goldfinches almost anywhere from northern Texas, Alabama, and the Carolinas to Manitoba, Quebec, and Newfoundland. For the winter there is a general move a few hundred miles southward, but even so, some individuals often brave the cold months as far north as the Border States east of the Rockies.

$\mathcal{R}$AVENS

GLOOMY AND BLACK, YET THEY FLY FOR FUN

There is little about a raven that makes you like it, as you may remember from your reading of Poe's famous poem. But somehow you are bound to feel a certain respect for the bird's ruggedness of body and spirit, despite the lugubrious appearance and the reputation for evil ways that always dogs it.

Superficially, ravens look like outsize crows with shaggy throat feathers, and they have a wingspread of about four feet. Instead of cawing, though, they croak and occasionally give an indescribable call that sounds almost like the ringing of a bell. They are superb fliers, too, characteristically interspersing hawk-like glides along with their wingbeats. At times they will tumble, dive, and roll high in the sky, apparently just for the fun of the thing. Another favorite diversion is fighting mock air battles with other big birds, easily outmaneuvering their opponents and, in their moody sort of way, enjoying the experience.

But despite these bursts of gaiety, or whatever you'd call them, raven nature is not too pleasant. The bird is a downright scavenger, you see, and will eat almost anything it can find, alive or long dead. Small wild animals, poultry, young lambs, offal, fish, eggs and young of other birds, garbage, reptiles, worms, insects, grains—these are only a few of its dishes. Like their cousin the crow, ravens are geniuses at locating food and digesting it. They even drop clams on the beach to crack them open, the way herring gulls do. And always ravens are smarter than smart when it comes to keeping their black selves out of serious trouble.

Despite all this, there are a few touches of gold underneath all those sable feathers. Ravens mate for life and are unfailingly devoted to their yearly brood of five or six, continuing to feed and look after them long after they are on the wing. The nest, a bulky affair of sticks three or four feet across, and well lined with softer stuff, is built on an inaccessible mountain ledge or high in a big forest tree, and the same pair often returns to the vicinity year after year. Egg-laying starts early in the season—the first part of April in Maine, for instance, and only a month later in northern Canada. To their credit be it said, the parents share the duties of incubation.

We have two almost identical ravens in this country: the northern, found chiefly in wilderness regions from northern Canada to Maine, Michigan, Minnesota, and sparingly southward through the mountains to Georgia; and the American, a bird of comparable areas in the West beyond the Dakotas. Both are year-round residents wherever you find them, and both resemble the ravens of the Old World.

CANADA JAY

CURIOSITY IS ITS WATCHWORD

Call it camp robber, whisky jack, meat hawk, moosebird, or just plain Canada jay—it's all the same to this black, white and two-tone gray cousin of our familiar blue jay. You might not think of it as even a distant relative were it not for an endless variety of call notes and the propensity for prying into all kinds of business besides its own, for the Canada jay is decidedly inconspicuous in color and its feathers are fluffy and often rumpled-looking. But if you were to go into the North Woods which are its home, whether in summer or winter, and became familiar with whisky jack's ways, you'd recognize the family traits only too well.

Canada jays are the scavengers of the northern forests. Apparently they see in the activities of men a splendid opportunity for filling their stomachs, for they will come boldly into camp and steal anything that looks as if it might be edible. Meat, plug tobacco, bread, fish, bits of soap, almost any loose article not too big to fly away with —all may be snatched from practically under your hand. Sometimes the plunder is eaten at once, again it is tucked into tree-bark crevices as if for future reference.

In winter the camp robbers will trail the trap lines, stealing the baits and sometimes feasting on any small animals that may have been caught and killed. To them, hunters appear to be food-providing friends rather than enemies, and some old woodsmen will tell you that the sound of a gunshot will bring whisky jacks promptly through the woods in the hope that it means more provender for them.

It is most unusual to find Canada jays south of New Brunswick and northern New England westward through the upper parts of the Border States. They do not definitely migrate, as do so many other birds, but spend all their time in the spruce forests of the North Country where, even while snow still lies deep on the ground, they build surprisingly neat nests of twigs, sphagnum moss, and bark shreds, well lined with feathers and other soft, warm materials.

Usually the site is rather near the ground and close to the trunk, where there is good branch support. The three or four eggs often hatch while temperatures still range below zero, and edible fresh food for the young is scarce. Under such circumstances the old birds fall back on the bits they hid in the bark crevices when times were easier, and with their aid are able to tide the kids over until more prosperous days return. Being real jays, though, and therefore equipped by Nature to adapt themselves to their environment, camp robbers do not tempt Providence too far by attempting more than one brood a year.

168

$\mathcal{R}$OAD-RUNNER

FANTASTIC SPRINTER OF THE DESERT

The fact that weird regions often have weird inhabitants is perfectly illustrated by the cactus country of our Southwest and the fantastic road-runners that live there. If you want complete novelty and fantastic change, be sure to see them both.

Road-runners are nearly two feet long, half of that length being devoted to a highly mobile tail whose main purpose appears to be that of a combined rudder and brake when its owner is twisting and dodging through the chaparral scrub which is so frequent in the regions the birds haunt. They are not much when it comes to flying, but how they can and do run—quite as fast as a man, and not far from the speed of a good horse. One look at their long, powerful legs and the slim, streamlined shape of the whole bird, and you realize where their incredible foot speed comes from.

Actually, the road-runner, or chaparral cock, is a completely amazing fellow from just about every standpoint. For example, it is inordinately fond of eating snakes, lizards, and small animals like mice, all of which it catches easily and kills speedily with its formidable bill. Grasshoppers, crickets, scorpions, and tarantulas are welcomed too, but William L. Finley, who made a close field study of road-runners, says that even the young are frequently fed on lizards almost from the time they are hatched. The technique, Mr. Finley reports, is for the old bird to kill the reptile and then push it head-first into the youngster's mouth. Sometimes the lizard is too long to be swallowed all at once, in which case its tail simply stays outside until the head end of the beast is sufficiently digested to make room for the rear section.

Road-runner nests are well-built flat collections of sticks lined with softer stuff, located in low trees or shrubs a few feet from the ground, and only three to six eggs are laid. Not too much is known about the parents' incubation habits, but it has been established that a single nest may contain a perfectly fresh egg, another well on its way to hatching, a couple of black, featherless young, and two others almost ready to leave. This certainly seems to point to widely spaced egg-laying and also to incubation beginning as soon as the first egg or two is deposited. Such a combination is rare among our wild birds, of course, and the reason for it is far from apparent. But then road-runners are a law unto themselves!

If you're looking for these half-clown characters, go to western Kansas or central Texas, on to Utah and California, and south as far as Mexico City. The time of year won't make much difference, for road-runners are permanent residents wherever you find them.

$\mathcal{P}$ELICANS

FIRST YOU LAUGH AND THEN YOU MARVEL

If the day should ever come when competent researchers delve into the reasons why people like Florida, I suspect that pelicans would prove to rate close to the citrus fruits, sunshine, and bathing-beauty beaches. Anyway, that's a fair deduction on the basis of the endless entertainment afforded by these huge, grotesque, and infinitely interesting birds.

A pelican, whether the common brown species or the western, much larger white, is a strange combination of ludicrous looks and amazingly competent actions. It is a master of flying and fishing skill, carrying its creel with it in the form of a distensible pouch under its comic-character bill. On foot it is as ungainly as any circus clown, but once fairly on the wing, there are few if any birds with such complete ability to utilize or defy every current and draft. The twenty- or thirty-foot headlong plunge of a brown into the ocean to capture a fish is one of the sights (and sounds) of the coast, almost as amazing as the skill with which a wing-to-wing line will glide for miles barely above the waves, with only an occasional flap to supplement the buoying effect of the air.

There is a popular belief that the main purpose of the pelican's bill pouch is that of a basket in which to carry home live fish for the kiddies to eat. This apparently is a misconception; in fact, on the very face of the situation, a pouchful of fresh fish could well overbalance even a flying giant like this fellow. Actually, the chief job of the pouch appears to be twofold. First to be a sort of scap net to catch small fish while the bird is swimming—a use which it particularly serves in the case of the non-diving white species—and second, a convenient receptacle for the regurgitated food on which the old birds actually feed their young. Were you to see the actual feeding operation you would notice that the youngsters reach into the pouch as eagerly as human small fry are supposed to head for a saucer of trade-named cereal.

Both brown and white pelicans are colony nesters, but today the non-migratory brown breeds only on the Atlantic side of the Americas from South Carolina to Brazil, and along the Gulf Coast. Here, among mangrove bushes or directly on the ground, it gathers sticks, weed stalks, and so on to serve as a bed for three white eggs, laid sometime between November and May.

The white species, on the other hand, is a more northern bird, nesting in fresh-water country from British Columbia eastward to Manitoba and south to the Dakotas, Utah, and southern California. For the winter, however, it takes to salt water, notably along the coasts of southern California, the Gulf States, Florida, Cuba, Mexico, and Costa Rica.

How big is a pelican? Well, a white may be nearly six feet long, weigh fifteen pounds, and spread nine feet from tip to tip. The brown, on the other hand, is a couple of feet shorter in both breadth and length, and weighs proportionately less. Neither, you see, is what you'd exactly call a little bird.

Burrowing Owl

IT NESTS IN THE GROUND AND NEVER HOOTS

As if to prove that owls don't always follow the strict party line, this little oddity of the West's wide open spaces nests in a hole in the ground, prefers daytime activity to night life, and instead of hooting says *cack-cack-cack* or, in the evening, *coo-hoo,* somewhat like a mourning dove. There is a popular belief, too, that the bird chooses a rattlesnake for an underground roommate, but when and if this does occur, it is more from chance than from preference.

Burrowing owls, like the land they live in, are far from being the gentle souls that their language and nine-inch length might indicate. They have exceedingly competent talons and beaks and will catch and eat almost anything from grasshoppers to gophers, snakes, lizards, and sometimes birds almost as big as they are. There is one authentic record of cannibalism, too—several young birds kept in confinement for a few days started to kill and eat each other.

During the daytime they spend much time standing at the entrance to their burrows, bowing and posturing as they survey the scene in all directions. Early morning and evening are their most active times, however—one of the few concessions they make toward the traditions of how well-bred owls should behave in the dark.

The nesting site is usually several feet inside an abandoned fox, gopher, or badger burrow, although this little owl is quite able to dig its own hole if the ground is loose. At the point where the nest is made the burrow is widened enough to make space for a collection of weed stalks or any other handy material in which the five to seven pure-white eggs are laid.

173

Burrowing owls are distinctly birds of unforested regions and are known to breed in southwestern Canada, South Dakota, Nebraska, and down through Kansas to Texas and Louisiana, as well as on the Pacific Coast through Lower California and Mexico to Guatemala and Panama. North of Kansas they are migratory, moving southward for the winter and returning in the spring. Elsewhere you may see them at any time of the year, if your eyes are good at spotting a little, long-legged, two-toned brown bird with partly whitish under parts standing on the ground or on a low fence post.

The central and lower Florida mainland has its native burrowing owl also—very similar to the western species but differing from it enough for the ornithologists to rate it as a subspecies. Here, as in the West, the place to look for your bird is on the open grasslands or prairies, where the sandy soil makes tunneling easy.

WOOD THRUSH

TOP SOLOIST OF LAWNS AND WOODLANDS

One back-country name for this outstanding member of the thrush clan is wood robin, and another is swamp angel—the former perhaps because it is pre-eminently a woods dweller nearly as large as a robin, and the latter in obvious reference to its predilection for moist localities and the ethereal quality of its song. Throughout its breeding range from Louisiana, Alabama, and Florida northward to Maine, Ontario, and Michigan there is no better-loved bird or one that ranks higher as a musician and aristocrat.

All our thrushes are fine singers, and there are those who rate the song of the hermit thrush above any other. But when a wood thrush lifts his serene, rich voice in the dusk of a May evening—well, how *could* anything be finer? I have heard both species sing many times in many places, and while the cadences of the hermit coming from the still depths of a North Country forest at nightfall are spiritual beyond all believing, it always seems to me that those of the wood reflect the serenity of the finer things of life as well as of heaven.

Yet perhaps that last statement should not be left unqualified, for not every male wood thrush possesses either the voice or the repertoire that have made his race so famous in the bird world. As with people, some individuals seem unable to sing beautifully, try as they will. Have their throats suffered some injury, or were they merely hatched that way? I wonder!

These handsome, russet-backed songsters arrive in the Middle

States sometime in April from their winter homes in southern Mexico and Central America and remain until October. Originally they were probably forest birds, and most of them still prefer wooded areas not far from water. On the other hand, they have become increasingly frequent around spacious home grounds, and you often see them after a summer shower hopping robin-wise about the lawns of a big estate where bordering shade trees and shrubbery afford the kind of nesting sites that they love so well. In such surroundings they find an abundance of their favorite insect foods, and they seldom abuse their privileges by robbing the fruit garden.

Wood thrushes locate their nests substantially in bushes or low tree branches, building them of grass, bark fibers, damp leaf mold that dries hard as mud does, and lining them with finer, softer materials of various kinds. Very often pieces of paper are woven into the structure, for no apparent reason and despite the fact that their light color could well catch the eye of some prowling marauder. The three or four eggs have the same distinctive greenish-blue color as a robin's (another of the thrush group, by the way), and generally only one brood a year is undertaken.

Of all the thrush group, only the robin and bluebird can compare with the wood thrush in friendliness and adaptability to human surroundings. It often nests within a few yards of your house, sometimes scarcely an arm's length away from a window. Only last year I knew of a pair that raised four perfectly healthy youngsters in a yew so close to a front door that every caller could look right down into their nest while he waited for someone to answer his ring. Not many birds would do that and remain perfectly calm about it for weeks!

You might not expect that a bird with such calmness and habitual serenity could become a scolding fighter, but there are occasions when a wood thrush does precisely that. Let a prowling cat or any other threat to bird life and happiness put in an appearance, and the erstwhile singer sounds off with a volley of vehement alarm notes that carry far and effectively. The gentlemanly, well-poised mood of a few moments ago vanishes completely, and in its place you see an alert, valiant spirit of defense that will risk almost any danger to attain its purpose.

$\mathscr{H}$ORNED $\mathscr{L}$ARK

OUR COUNTERPART OF EUROPE'S SKYLARK

Most of the lark family, including the famous European skylark, live in the Old World, but the self-possessed little character which is the subject of this sketch is a regular native-born American. The first half of its name, as the illustration suggests, comes from the two pointed feather tufts on its head which, when raised, really look like tiny horns. Actually there are numerous slightly varying forms of the species in different parts of the country.

There is a good bit of the skylark about the song and form of this hardy and distinctive seven-incher. The unusually long hind toe, a special adaptation to the largely pedestrian life both species lead, is one similarity. Another is the habit of singing while on the wing, a high, tinkling, and infectious outpouring that often continues for a surprisingly long time. And both birds are strong if somewhat erratic fliers that seem to find sheer delight in darting through the air as the spirit moves them.

Horned larks are birds of the open, wind-swept country, choosing barren areas where there is no brush and little if any grass. Their breeding grounds are from the Arctic to North Carolina, West Virginia, Kansas, Missouri, and the Texas coast. They, or one of their subspecies, can be found throughout this huge territory, except the Canadian portion, in every month of the year, for the birds can be classified as winter wanderers rather than true migrants.

In the eastern part of its range the horned lark is so largely a seacoast bird that it used to be called shore lark. Beaches, sand dunes, blocks of winter ice, miles of snow-covered flats—these are its haunts, regardless of the weather. You wonder how such bleak territory can yield sufficient food for birds whose diet, in the over-all picture, is made up of about twenty per cent insects and eighty per cent seeds and other vegetal matter. But if larks could talk, they'd probably say that they know their business much better than we do. One answer, no doubt, is their constant walking or trotting about, which takes them into a lot of territory in the course of a day.

Horned lark nests are simple cups of grasses, feathers, and other soft stuff set in a slight depression of the bare ground. Often they are right out in the open, at other times close to a rock or clump of dead seaweed. On occasion they have been known to nest in such unexpected spots as college campuses and beach-club parking lots, though of course such confidence in mankind is the exception rather than the rule.

Nesting begins so early in the spring that the whole project may be wrecked by a snowstorm, but horned larks are not discouraged by anything as simple as that and merely start all over again. Four greenish, brown-speckled eggs are the normal complement, and the male birds seem to leave the whole incubation task to their mates.

$\mathscr{W}$INTER $\mathscr{W}$REN

TINIEST AND TOUGHEST OF ITS TRIBE

Most of us think of wrens as being essentially home-grounds birds of the spring and summer months, but unless you live in Canada or the northern Border States, or southward in the higher portions of the Alleghenies and their adjacent ranges, you are unlikely to see this smallest of the tribe except in the colder months. Its winter home is chiefly from the latitude of central Ohio to the Gulf Coast, a far cry indeed from the cold northern forests where it usually nests.

This little scrap of a bird is the smallest of our American wrens, and in many ways the most interesting. When you are lucky enough to catch a glimpse of its tubby wee form skipping about a jumble of woodland rocks or tree roots, it suggests a brown, barred ping-pong ball with an absurdly short tail sticking straight up in the air. It's a case of now you see it and now you don't, for the bird loves to disappear into a hole or crevice and pop out again a yard or more away. It is such a confirmed skulker and hider that, together with those quick movements and dark, incredibly protective coloring, you might almost think it a mouse. But no mouse ever had such an amusing tail or gave voice to so many wren-like scoldings and chatterings and short, sharp *chips*.

It is hard to conceive of so diminutive a bird, with such apparent unwillingness to take wing, managing a migration of a thousand miles or more every fall and spring, but the winter wren does precisely that. It starts the northward journey early, too, for the schedule calls for nesting to commence in northern New Hampshire or Maine, for example, soon after the middle of May. That means early

spring up there, and the secluded forests where winter wrens breed are still chilly. Yet the early start is easier to understand when you realize that two broods of young are to be raised before the time comes for all to move south again.

The nest is typically wren-like in its utilization of twigs, moss, and rootlets with feathers or fur for inner lining, but its location in a brush pile, tangle of fallen trees, or in the hollow of a stump or log is quite different from the ones chosen by our more familiar house wren. Six to ten eggs are laid, and the mother bird is believed to take full charge of hatching them, after which her mate does his fair share of providing food for the youngsters.

It is only in these cool forest surroundings that you are likely to hear the tinkly, bubbling, and astonishingly loud and varied song of this secretive little bird. Into it he seems to pour all his energy, his devotion to the wilderness, his abounding good spirits. Hear it even once and you will be coldhearted indeed if you don't choose the winter as your favorite of all the wrens.

$\mathscr{B}$LACK-POLL $\mathscr{W}$ARBLER

BRAZIL IN WINTER, ALASKA IN SUMMER

One does not ordinarily think of wood warblers as being particularly persistent, long-range travelers, but the black-poll is certainly an exception to any such generalization as that. Though scarcely over five inches long, and possessed of a singing voice so thin and high that you could well mistake it for some small insect's, this white and grayish streaked mite with the black topknot migrates twice a year between northern South America and the limits of its breeding range in northwestern Alaska, Ungava, Labrador, and Newfoundland. A long journey, indeed, and all the more remarkable in that virtually every black-poll that takes it enters and leaves North America by way of the Florida peninsula, which involves a four-hundred-mile water jump between a stopover respite on the island of Jamaica and the South American coast. Some travel via the Bahamas, but even that route is not exactly one for a fainthearted bird to take.

It is fairly late in the spring when the peak of this abundant warbler's immigration leaves Florida and spreads fanwise across the

States in the direction of the Far Northern evergreen forests where the species breeds. There, almost up to the Arctic Circle in some instances, the pairs build snug nests of lichens, grass, twigs, and moss, line them with still softer materials, and provide for posterity with four or five creamy, variegated little eggs. The site is usually low in a spruce or other conifer, and the more stunted and dense the tree the better.

In late August the southward trek begins, and by September the birds are passing through the States. But you might not recognize the males now, for their black caps have vanished and an olive-green cast over all their plumage has dulled the definite markings of springtime.

Not too much is known of the black-poll's feeding habits, though it is established that it consumes vast numbers of cankerworms, aphids, and webworms. Beyond question it is one of our most useful birds during the comparatively short time it is with us, and certainly its benefits are spread over a tremendous territory. It takes a lot of food to sustain even a little bird through such lengthy journeys, and black-polls really know how to catch it for their own well-being and, secondarily, for ours.

*B*ARN *O*WL

DWELLER IN BELFRIES AND TOWERS

Lord Tennyson may not have been as famous a bird-watcher as he was a poet, but the odds are about ten to one that he had the barn owl in mind when he wrote

> *Alone and warming his five wits,*
> *The white owl in the belfry sits.*

That's just the kind of place these monkey-faced fellows choose for their base of operations against the neighborhood rats and mice, even on the outskirts of some of our large modern cities; and though

they are not strictly white, they come close enough to earn that description with a little allowance for poetic license.

There are almost thirty forms of barn owls, widely distributed around the world except in the colder regions. Here in the States we have only one, but you may find that single species almost anywhere from Massachusetts, Ohio, and Wisconsin south to the Gulf of Mexico, as well as in the West from Oregon into Mexico. As a rule, though, you won't get a good view of the bird unless you discover it during the daytime in its nesting or roosting retreat, for it becomes active only after dark. This hide-out may be in an abandoned barn, a church tower, a cavity in a big tree, or even a hole in a high bank. At least one pair that I knew utilized the second-floor fireplace openings in several large brick chimneys which marked the site of a New Jersey mansion destroyed by fire many years before. Another more famous nesting place was in a tower of the Smithsonian Institution in Washington, D.C.

But though you may never see a barn owl in the flesh, hearing one at night is by no means unusual. Its commonest note is a weird, rasping sort of snore—unpleasant enough, but mild indeed compared with the less frequent scream which makes your hair stand on end.

Nest-building is a simple matter with barn owls: they just don't bother to do any, except as they may gather together some of the trash which happens to be on the floor of the retreat they have chosen. Here the female lays her half-dozen or so unmarked, whitish eggs from which, about three weeks later, emerge downy white young whose heads and bills, at this stage, resemble those of a vulture much more than an owl. A nestful of owlets often presents a surprising variety of sizes, because the eggs are laid several days apart and incubation apparently starts when the first one is deposited. Breeding time in the North is usually in fairly early spring, but July to May is the period in Florida.

Barn owls are not really migratory, though they are likely to wander southward in winter from their breeding places. On the other hand, some move farther north in summer and fall when their young have left the nest. So perhaps, in addition to their other oddities, it is reasonable to call them just erratic explorers.

$\mathscr{S}$ONG $\mathscr{S}$PARROW

EVERYONE'S DOORYARD FAVORITE

Most kinds of birds are somewhat aloof toward mankind, but song sparrows are definitely of the companionable type. They seem to like living close to human habitations, and their springtime singing from lilac bush or grape trellis is one of the cheeriest ways they have of showing it. Another is the frequency with which they build their quite bulky nests of grass stems and leaves, lined with softer stuff, in a barberry or other dense shrub or vine literally within arm's length of your window. Four or five eggs are the usual complement, and it is not at all unusual for three broods to be raised in a single season.

Habits often are the clue to a bird's name, and so the song sparrow's appellation comes from the cheerfulness and persistence of his singing. He tunes up on pleasant days even in late winter, and it is autumn before he calls it quits for the year. During the height of the spring he is likely to sing as often as eight times a minute, and sometimes you hear him even in the middle of the night. I think it was Thoreau who translated the song sparrow's typical spring song as "Maids! maids! maids! hang up your teakettle-ettle-ettle!"

No land bird is more fond of bathing; often it will splatter around in your pool even after sunset, though it may have been there a dozen times during the day. The bird really gets wet, too, and sometimes I have seen it literally spread itself out to dry in the sun after a particularly thorough session in the water. In the event of a local shortage, song sparrows still manage a tub or two by fluttering in wet leaves or grass after a shower.

This unquenchable and likable little bundle of optimism is very widely distributed—actually it breeds throughout North America east of the Rockies and from well up in the Canadian Provinces to north Georgia and Missouri. To a considerable extent it is migratory, but it does not go really all out in moving either north or south as the seasons change. In winter you will find it as far south as the Gulf of Mexico, but if you look in sheltered, brushy nooks and corners in New England during January and February, you are likely to find some song sparrows there too.

These notes on distribution apply to the song sparrow as most of us know it. Actually the ornithologists say that there are some twenty-three geographical races of this species, all but two of them found in areas west of the region we have been discussing. Basically they are one and the same species, the variations being chiefly in size and color. Those in the Southwest are generally paler and smaller than their representatives of the North. The race found in Mexico, for example, is only six inches long, while the much darker one native to the Aleutian Islands measures almost nine inches. The desert song sparrow, found in the Colorado Desert, is so pale that you'd think it a distinct species.

The reasons for all these variations of a single species? Well, perhaps the best way to sum them up is to say that they represent special adaptations to particular surroundings and climates. After all, life in the Colorado Desert just has to be different from that in a New Jersey suburban garden.

$\mathscr{P}$RAIRIE $\mathscr{C}$HICKEN

BIRD SYMBOL OF THE OLD WEST

The prairie chicken, one of the showiest of the grouse tribe, is a bird of the great open spaces from Indiana, Illinois, Arkansas, and Missouri west and north to Manitoba and Saskatchewan; a few are found, too, in southern Texas and Louisiana. It is a big, hearty bird, as much as eighteen inches long and weighing up to two pounds, beautifully patterned with black, white, and brown bars. Were you to see one walking about on the ground you would immediately think of a peculiarly neat, nicely marked chicken.

These prairie lovers are chicken-like, also, in their habit of nesting in slight depressions on the ground with only a thin layer of grasses and maybe a few feathers between the soil and their eight to a dozen buffy eggs. Nor does the similarity to fowls end there, for the downy, animated-toy chicks can run about as soon as they are dry after emerging from their shells, and soon learn to garner the countless seeds and ground insects on which their elders subsist.

The most spectacular period in prairie chicken life comes every spring with the advent of the courtship season. Many years ago it was so graphically described by the late Dr. Frank M. Chapman that I take the liberty of quoting his account as it appeared in *Birds of America:*

"On frosty spring mornings, as the sun rises over the prairies, one may at times hear a singular, resonant, booming note, *boom-ah-b-o-o-m, boom-ah-b-o-o-m.* It is the love-song of the prairie hen. He may be near at hand or possibly two miles away, so far does this sound, unobstructed by tree or hill, carry in the clear air. It is well worth following, however, for we may find the maker of it, with perhaps ten to fifty of his kind, engaged in a most remarkable performance.

"During the mating season, from March until early in May, the prairie hens of a certain district or area gather before daybreak to take part in these courtship demonstrations. The feather tufts on either part of the neck are erected like horns, the tail raised and spread, the wings drooped, when the bird first rushes forward a few steps, pauses, inflates its orange-like air sacs, and with a violent, jerking, muscular effort produces the startling boom which we may have heard when two miles distant. At other times, with a low cackle, he springs suddenly into the air, as though quite unable to control himself, and finally he comes within striking distance of a rival who has been giving a similar exhibition. Then, with much clashing of wings, a fight ensues which often strews the nearby grass with feathers. These tournaments of display and combat are doubtless designed to arouse the attention of the females, but they also occur when only males are present. Within an hour or two after sunrise, the time varying with the ardor of the birds, the competition is over for the day and the rivals feed peacefully together, until they enter the lists the following morning."

$\mathscr{P}$IED-BILLED $\mathscr{G}$REBE

IT LIVES IN THE WATER BUT NEVER GETS WET

Dabchick, hell-diver, water-witch—these are a few of the names by which this unique little water bird is known in the North American part of its vast range, which extends all the way from the Canadian Provinces to Chile, Argentina, and occasionally even to Cape Horn. As we know it in the North, it is a haunter of fresh-water ponds and sluggish streams fringed with cattails and other aquatic plants among which it can find food, refuge, and concealment for its bulky floating nest of dead rushes, reeds, and other vegetal trash, often enough to fill a bushel basket. Large though it is, the inside of the nest is seldom dry, because its materials are constantly half water-logged.

Indeed, the bird itself would be soaked to the skin most of the time were it not for the compact, half-hairy character of its plumage and the fact that all the feathers are kept well waterproofed with oil spread by means of their wearer's bill from glands located on the rump. The net result is that a grebe never hesitates to pop under water and swim about in search of food or to escape from danger, traveling with surprising speed by the simple process of using wings as well as feet for propellers. If you follow one in a canoe and drive it into shallow water, you are likely to see it doubling back toward the channel faster than you could paddle, perhaps passing directly under your craft.

On the surface, grebes float quite high and buoyantly when at ease, but if uneasy, they will sink gradually lower until only their heads are above the surface. The degree of submersion is under perfect control, due partly to air sacs connected with the lungs which can be filled or emptied at will. Whether floating high or low, a grebe's dive is the essence of ease and suddenness. In the days of flintlock guns

Don Eckelberry

men said that the little birds could disappear in the moment between the flash of powder in the pan and the arrival of the shot—a claim that may well have been literally true.

The length of time that a grebe can stay completely under water has never been determined, I believe, partly because its natural surroundings doubtless give it numerous opportunities to raise its head cautiously above the surface where the water weeds grow thickly and breathe freely without its whereabouts becoming known. Where the birds were feeding normally in open water, with no concealing marsh growths within reach, I have known them to remain fully submerged for a full two minutes, and the chances are that they can hold their breath considerably longer than that if they want to. Under such unfrightened conditions their diving motions are fascinating to watch—not a real dive, as we think of such things, but rather an incredibly smooth, effortless headfirst disappearance so ludicrous that "ploop" is about the only way to describe it.

The family life of these extraordinary "water-witches" is as remarkable as their other characteristics. Usually the female lays from four to eight bluish-white eggs, and she and her mate take turns incubating them for three weeks or so in their dank bed. If frightened away, the old bird instantly scatters trash over them with bill or wings and dives overboard like a shot. If your eyes were keen enough you would probably see it streak away under water to a nearby tangle of rushes, where it would cautiously rise just enough to bring its bill and eyes above the surface and motionlessly watch you.

The young take to the water soon after they hatch and quickly learn to dive like their parents. Frequently several of them ride around on the old bird's back, partly hidden among the feathers, and when she or he dives, they go under too. It is said, also, that sometimes they get a submerged ride by hanging to Mom's tail feathers with their bills—a quite probable performance.

As for vocal attainments, grebes have several loud, rapidly repeated calls on the general theme of *cow-cow-cow, keggy-keggy-keggy, wah-hoo, wah-hoo, wah-hoo,* or *kuck-kuck-kuck.* In fact, any way you choose to take them, they are as amazing as just about any bird you could name.

MOCKINGBIRD

MOSTLY YOU'LL LOVE HIM, BUT——

Most people who know mockingbirds well—which means those who have spent much time south of the Mason-Dixon line, as that is the mocker's chief territory—are of two minds about them. On the credit side are bodily grace, a lovely color scheme of soft grays and white, fearlessness in defending its nest and young, and a song that is full, rich, and incredibly varied. But when that loud, repetitive refrain continues incessantly not only day after day but night after night when you are trying to get to sleep—well, sometimes it's just a little too much!

Mockingbirds are year-round residents southward from Maryland, Ohio, Illinois, and occasional individuals are scattered considerably north and east of this territory. They appear to be non-migratory in much of the area where you find them, and seem to be gradually extending their range eastward. Strong and self-reliant, they have no difficulty in withstanding a lower New England winter provided there is a good supply of wild berries and hibernating insects.

A mockingbird courtship is something to see. Its first antic is when the male, on his singing perch high in a tree, pauses in his song to stretch his wings high over his head, presumably to impress the lady with the beauty of his conspicuous white patches. As the affair proceeds both birds go through a sort of formal dance, heads and tails held high while they face each other and solemnly hop from side to side or in circles.

Mockers build substantial nests of almost anything they can pick up, from twigs to weeds, grass, rags, feathers, bark, and string, locating them usually in a dense shrub, tree, or vine anywhere from one

to fifty feet from the ground. The males do some of the materials-carrying work, but most of the construction falls on the ladies. Two and sometimes three clutches a year are the rule, a total of perhaps ten to fifteen bluish-green eggs blotched with reddish brown.

You can hardly call the mockingbird a lovable character—it is rather too masterful and combative for that. But the male is a master of the voice and has been known to change his tune eighty-seven times in seven minutes. Many of his notes are imitations of the calls and songs of other birds, often modified according to the mocker's own ideas. Frequently, too, he picks up such sounds as a rooster's crow, the barking of a dog, even the squeak of a rusty gate hinge. With so much to express, and so tireless a voice in which to express it, you are not surprised to see him sometimes flutter high into the air while he pours out his song, as if buoyed up by its sheer pressure.

$\mathcal{P}$URPLE $\mathcal{M}$ARTIN

TENEMENT GOSSIP AND MASTER OF SMALL TALK

Martins are the tenement gossips of the bird world. They like to live in colonies, with the result that a multiple-compartment birdhouse made especially for them and mounted on a tall pole may be occupied by a dozen or more pairs, all raising their families and having a gorgeous time chattering with each other from their respective doorways and perches. Unlike people, though, their gossiping never seems to lead to serious feuds; each family attends to its own business, and so the community is cheerful and happy. But woe betide any marauder that dares approach, for the whole crowd is likely to gang up on him in a jiffy.

In appearance, flight, and general habits, purple martins are over-size swallows—dark steel-blue and black in the case of the males, duller and more grayish if they are females. Originally they probably nested in tree cavities, and no doubt often appropriated old woodpecker holes. But as far back as we have records they seem to have been favorites of mankind, for the Indians used to hang hollowed gourds on saplings to provide nesting places for them, a practice that is still followed by many Negroes in the Southern States. Once a few pairs decide to settle in one colony, they will return to it year after year, probably accompanied by some of their previous season's young, so the group may gradually increase to surprising size.

Martin small talk is as varied as it is incessant. When a colony is in full activity around its apartment house, swooping, fluttering, constantly coming and going, the air is filled with an amazing mixture of chirrups, squeaks, whistles, and trills, all uttered with engaging heartiness. The excitement is still greater after the eggs hatch, for then the parent birds are constantly arriving with food for their four or five offspring—dragonflies, butterflies, and all manner of flying insects—and the squeaks of the ever-hungry young are added to the general tumult. What it must be like in all those grass, feather, and mud nests inside the community house is something to imagine almost with awe.

It is believed that purple martins used to be birds of the Tropics and eventually spread northward largely because of their great powers of flight. Certainly they succumb easily to periods of wet, cold weather during which insects are hard to find, a fact which accounts in part for their comparative rarity today in New England and some other northern areas. A second factor, no doubt, is the occupation of many of their nesting places by the imported English sparrow, which starts its own housekeeping before the martins arrive in April from their winter quarters in Brazil. In any event, the Southern States are *the* place to find purple martins nowadays, and many a northern bird-watcher has never seen even one.

BLUE JAY

BEAUTIFUL AND BRASH

In some ways the blue jay reminds me of Rhett Butler in *Gone with the Wind:* it's so handsome, capable, brash—and rascally. Also it is the most resourceful of all our everyday native birds, with the exception of a not-too-distant black cousin, the crow. In whatever part of the country you find blue jays, there they stay the year through, scorning to migrate.

Maybe you don't like jays. A good many people feel that way, for there's no denying that these birds are noisy, omnivorous, rob other birds' nests of eggs and sometimes, perhaps, of the newly hatched young. But only a confirmed hater could help admiring their showy blue, white, and black plumage, their high spirit in facing the toughest conditions the weatherman can throw at them, the endless posturings and flirtings and crest-raisings and cheerful conversations with which they go about their daily affairs. They are at once the dandies and the daredevils of the bird world, and—well, I like them!

If you want to see the blue jay at its spectacular best, watch one as, with a dozen of its kind, it comes trooping in for an accustomed feeding station breakfast soon after sunup on a cold winter morning. The group arrives singly and yet together, a straggling flock flaunting from tree to nearer tree, calling back and forth in strident but not unpleasing voices, varied sometimes by double-note flutings as soft and musical as bird ever uttered. From a high branch the foremost drops to the feeder with a flourish of spread tail and wings gleaming in the sunshine, snatches a sunflower seed or bit of suet, and flashes away to a nearby branch to eat it. One after another the rest follow its lead, and soon the air is a circus ground of gorgeous flying acrobats so adroit and confident in every motion that you can scarcely believe your eyes. The big show holds its climax for some minutes, then gradually slackens as bird after bird eats its fill. Finally the flock departs as it came, seeking interests elsewhere.

Such is the blue jay in those free and roving months from September into March. Then, with April, come quieter, more serious days when you hardly ever see and still more rarely hear one. The pairs are thinking of family matters now, and the old gang life becomes a thing of the past. So secretive do the birds become that a pair may nest, hatch, and raise their four or five young no more than a hundred feet from the house without your being aware of their presence. Often their stout twig nest is hidden in an evergreen tree or a thickly leaved oak or other deciduous sort. In any event, the parent birds approach and leave it furtively and in complete silence. Faced with the age-old duty of producing and protecting posterity, the noisy freebooters of yesterday have changed to the skulkers of today— easily, without fuss or fuming, as becomes birds that are such master strategists.

$\mathcal{C}$ANADA $\mathcal{G}$OOSE

SKIRMISH LINES ACROSS THE SKY

To many thousands of people across the United States the Canada goose is the most spectacular and legendary of all our birds. Country folk know it as the real harbinger of spring and the true prophet of approaching winter. As soon as the ice goes out the geese follow its melting northward, winging high and strongly, sometimes fifty or more, in a tenuous skirmish line led by an old gander wise in the ways and dangers of travel and rigidly insistent on obedience to his honked orders. Virtually wing-to-wing they go, each a little behind and out from the bird ahead, so that the whole flock is in a blunt V-shaped formation trailing back on either side of the leader's post at its point.

Though generations of country folk have known that every sizable flock of migrating Canada geese has an acknowledged leader, it is only within comparatively recent years that the true reason for the wing-to-wing formation of the group has been understood. It now appears that it is primarily a matter of practical aerodynamics, each bird benefiting by its relation to the slipstream, as it were, from the body and wing of the bird next to and slightly ahead of it. If you watch the passing of such a flock you will notice frequently that its precise formation seems unstable, varying between a broad V shape and an almost straight, though wavering single line. This may well be the result of a "bumpy" air condition where rigid adherence to the traditional V would be a disadvantage rather than a benefit. But this you will notice, too: whatever the changes in the line itself, the principle of staying just behind and to one side of the fellow next to you is almost always followed. If this makes you suspect that Nature has a functional reason for everything she does, you could hardly be more correct.

There is plenty of talking in the ranks as the birds sweep steadily forward—a sort of honking gabble that seems meaningless to us but no doubt is of real significance in the goose world. Save for the weird "laughter" of a loon on some northern lake, I know of no birdcall so completely thrilling, so filled with the spirit of the wilderness.

Canada geese breed as far away as the borders of the Barren Grounds in northern Canada, in Labrador, and to a lesser extent in the United States as far down as the Dakotas, Nevada, and northeastern California. Their winters are spent from the latitude of middle New England south to the Gulf Coast, so that over a large part of the country you may see occasional birds at almost any time of the year.

They are big birds, occasionally reaching a wingspread of over five feet and a weight of fourteen pounds, and they often have big families—anywhere from five to nine. Their nests are usually on dry ground near water, quite bulky affairs composed of twigs, weeds, reeds, and so on, softly lined with down. Both parents, which customarily mate for life, are as completely devoted to the eggs and young as they are to each other, and will stop at nothing to protect their dependents. The female does all the incubation of the one yearly brood while the male stands guard. He is a most efficient protector, too, and so fearless and powerful that he is said to be able to stand off a fox or even a deer that he thinks is coming too close for safety. If you have ever had the uncomfortable experience of being beaten up by an ordinary domestic gander, you can imagine how much more formidable a defender this bold, tough wild fellow can be.

During the spring and summer Canada geese feed freely on large insects, along with a variety of plant leaves, seeds, berries, and even roots. Later, when the insects are largely gone, their place may be partially taken by small crustaceans of different sorts, but even in midwinter the chief food seems to be vegetal.

203

$\mathscr{G}$OLDEN $\mathscr{P}$LOVER

THE OCEAN IS ITS FLYWAY

This stocky, robin-length shore bird with the black underbody in
spring and gold-flecked dusky back is one of our best long-distance
migrants and holds the overwater endurance flying championship
as far as land and semi-land birds are concerned. It is indeed a long
jump from Nova Scotia to the northern coast of South America, but

thousands of golden plovers make it non-stop every autumn on the way from the breeding grounds on the Arctic Coast and islands to their winter resort in southwestern Brazil and the La Plata River area. For weeks before they take off over the Atlantic they have fed to fatness on land insects and the little crowberries that grow so abundantly along the northeastern coasts, and presumably have stored up fuel to carry them to the mainland a little above the Equator, for many apparently do not stop off even at the Lesser Antilles Islands.

That is their southward course, a bold one indeed for a bird with webless feet and therefore unable to swim. But for reasons still unexplained the return journey in spring is much more of a land expedition—diagonally across South America to Panama, thence up through Central America to Yucatan, across the Gulf of Mexico, and so up through the central part of the continent to the Arctic.

Mid-June to early July is the season when these swift, intrepid little fliers are busy with homemaking in the Barren Grounds and tundra country of the Far North. Their nests are nothing to boast about—merely slight depressions in the earth lined with a few grasses, leaves, and the like. There is time for only one brood, of course, for the season is short up there and the young birds must be ready to start for the South not later than the end of August. The incubation period for the four or five olive-buff heavily spotted eggs is fairly long, but the parent birds share the duty with typical plover devotion. Presumably they are equally good providers of insect nutriment after the little goldens break out of their shells, for the young birds must grow fast and strongly—or else.

Many years ago, when the dwindling hosts of the passenger pigeon forced the market-gunners to turn to other species for a livelihood, these free-spirited little plovers were killed by countless thousands during their migration flights, a crime all the more easily committed because their compact traveling flocks and unsuspicious nature made it possible for many to be brought down with a single charge of shot. At one point they were dangerously close to extermination, but happily that day has passed and now, along with many others of the shore-bird group, their numbers are increasing once more.

WHITE-BREASTED NUTHATCH

OUR CHAMPION UPSIDE-DOWN BIRD

A young farmer neighbor of mine, untrained in the niceties of ornithology but, like many countrymen, keenly observant of its facts, calls the white-breasted nuthatch "that upside-down bird." No name could be more appropriate, for this nuthatch, at least during waking hours, spends fully as much time with its head lower than its tail as it does in a more conventional position. Why the bird seems to think no more about running headfirst down a vertical tree trunk than of climbing straight up it is doubtless its own affair. To us it looks fool-hardy and provocative of cerebral hemorrhages. But nobody has ever seen a nuthatch come to grief that way!

This trim little scrap of light gray, black, and white with a touch of rusty around its tummy has the special build and temperament of an all-around acrobat. Watch one closely as it searches a nearby tree for insects or gyrates comically at your feeding station while snatching a bit of suet or a sunflower seed, and you will notice how perfectly its legs, with their unusually long-toed feet, are designed to give full stability to the body weight regardless of position. That longish, pointed bill, too, has a rakish upward slant which, together with the backward tilt of the head when upside down, enables a nuthatch to look literally straight out at the world if it wants to. There is no long tail to get in the way while its owner scrambles about with apparent disregard for all the laws of gravity and safety. The bird is so stocky and perfectly balanced that a somersault means no more to it than a mere flip of a wing.

With it all, the white-breasted nuthatch is remarkably calm and matter-of-fact. You feel that it has a strong streak of friendliness toward people, too, and no little curiosity about them and their strange ways. With patience you can coax one to take a peanut from your fingers in winter when the hardships of cold and dwindling natural food supply make the birds constant visitors to the feeding

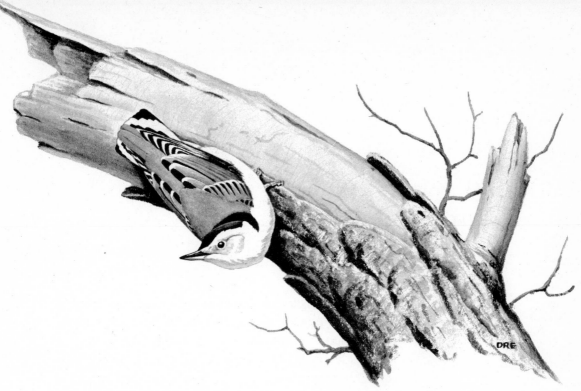

tray or suet holder. Speaking in a purely figurative sense, they always maintain a level head, carrying their nonchalance even to the point of not bothering to migrate like so many other birds. Wherever you find them, from Quebec to Florida, they stay around and take care of their own affairs from year's end to year's end. The name, incidentally, comes from the birds' habit of tucking acorns and other nut-like foods in bark crevices as provision against hard times.

At times the white-breasteds seem to display almost showmanship instincts, some of them endlessly amusing. At the feeding station they resort to all manner of seriocomic gestures calculated to frighten away other birds, raising their wings and dropping their heads threateningly as though about to tear the other fellow to shreds. Again, as the time approaches to start spring housekeeping in old woodpecker holes and similar cavities, the males court the ladies with fantastic gallantry, even going so far as to shell sunflower seeds for them and hand them the delectable kernels. Later, while the female broods the six or eight white, lightly spotted eggs which comprise the single annual clutch, her mate devotedly brings her food. Indeed, nuthatch family spirit is so strong that after the kids leave the nest the whole group, young and old, travels around together for weeks and sometimes even through the following winter.

PEREGRINE

THE FASTEST BIRD THAT FLIES

Any bird that inhabits every continent of the world is entitled to fame, and one that is capable of probably faster flight than all the rest has a clear claim to distinction. Small wonder, then, that the peregrine, or duck hawk, holds such an exalted position among bird-minded people, for it qualifies in both of these conditions as well as in a good many other important ones that have followed it through the centuries.

This long-winged, freebooting master of flight is perhaps the most noted of the highly specialized hawks that made falconry the top sport of seventeenth-century kings. Its ordinary cruising speed ranges from forty to sixty miles an hour, but when it dives or "stoops" to strike another flying bird with devastating force it is believed to reach a two-hundred-mile clip and perhaps a good deal more. Lest you wonder why such speed through the free air does not burst the bird's lungs, remember that a peregrine's nostrils are said to be equipped with a series of baffles which slow down the wind's velocity to that of a mere breeze.

Whenever you see a peregrine in flight you are impressed by its perfect design for the kind of life it leads. There is not a clumsy line in its contour, nor the least suggestion of looseness or superfluity anywhere. The whole body effect is torpedo-like—blunt, rounded head, short neck, sturdy shoulders that taper flawlessly to the tip of a moderately long tail. The legs and feet, if you are close enough to see them at all, are held close against the body so as not to retard its progress through the air, like the retracted wheels of a modern plane. And in competent support of all these physical assets, there

is a sense of vital driving power, with ample held in reserve for instant use, that pervades every quick, vigorous stroke of those superb wings and makes you realize that you are in the presence of one of the bird world's great leaders.

In the Western Hemisphere peregrines range over most of North and South America, though nowhere are they really abundant. With us they are somewhat migratory, so that in winter you are not likely to find them north of Colorado, Indiana, New Jersey, and Massachusetts. Wherever they go, their primary food is birds, ranging in size from snow buntings to the largest ducks and grouse. Domestic pigeons are a favorite prey, and in search for them a peregrine will often invade our largest cities, apparently undismayed by the skyscrapers and general din.

The customary nesting site is on a high mountain ledge, often overlooking a lake or stream. Here, in early spring, from two to six rich chocolate-brown eggs are laid and fiercely defended by both parents against any and all comers. Male and female share the duties of incubation, too, and the subsequent gathering of fresh bird meat such as they themselves eat. By the time the young birds are old enough to fly, the nest site is well sprinkled with a collection of bones and feathers that amply prove the character of the baby food they have been eating.

It is a far cry indeed from such a wild, secluded home to a high building ledge in the heart of a big city like Montreal or New York, but peregrines are known to nest in these super-sophisticated spots, presumably drawn to them by the abundance of town pigeons. Wherever the site may be, it is used year after year for a long time, quite possibly by the same pair.

These famous falcons are among the boldest, most capable and self-possessed birds in the world. To see one maneuvering easily for position a hundred feet above a desperately speeding pigeon is to witness the perfection of air-confidence. Then, with the beeline power dive, the devastating strike, and the calm flight to a favorite feeding spot with the dead quarry gripped in those long-hooked talons, there comes a feeling of mingled awe and admiration such as no other bird can inspire.

$\mathscr{N}$IGHTHAWK

THE BIRD WITH "HOLES" IN ITS WINGS

It really isn't a hawk, but a bug-eating cousin of the purely insectivorous whip-poor-will; and it certainly does not restrict its activities
to the dark hours. But because it flies high on long wings, and is

likely to be especially noticeable in the late afternoon and evening of warm days when large numbers of flying insects are abroad, men have been calling it nighthawk for many, many years.

A listing of the nighthawk's oddities contains strange facts. It ranges in migration over an enormous area from southern South America to the Arctic Ocean, but breeds only from the Gulf States northward. On the under side of each long wing both males and females have a round white spot which, seen against the sky, looks like an open hole. The male, when courting, performs weird aerial evolutions which culminate in a headlong dive that ends with a loud booming noise made by the air rushing through the large wing feathers as he turns sharply upward just before reaching the ground.

His mate builds no nest, but merely lays her two protectively colored eggs on bare ground, gravel, the top of a rock, or the flat, graveled roof of a city office building or apartment house. When brooding, she sits close, relying on her marvelous pattern of marbled grays, buffs, and blacks to conceal her presence; if this fails, she is likely to try bluffing an intruder by advancing with wide-open mouth and a series of cat-like spits and snakish hissings. Why her eggs are not baked or the young birds broiled by the intense summer sun beating down on their exposed position is at once a tribute to their toughness and a marvel to our mere human minds.

Since they feed exclusively on flying insects, from mosquitoes to large night-flying moths, nighthawks have enormous mouths that open far back under their ears—even farther than those of the swallows. The birds' considerable size (the wingspread is close to two feet), plus the fact that they are almost constantly in the air, calls for a huge consumption of food, so their stomachs are quite on a par with the capacity of their mouths. And finally, when a nighthawk occasionally decides to light on a tree branch, it sits lengthwise of it instead of crosswise like other birds.

One thing the nighthawk cannot do, and that is sing. It apparently has only one note, an utterly unmusical *spee-yah* or *bee-ak,* curiously nasal in quality. But it is extraordinarily proud of that call, judging by its frequent repetition as the bird hawks erratically about the sky in its incessant search for food.

$\mathcal{O}$VENBIRD

IT BUILDS A ROOF OVER ITS HEAD

Most of the wood warblers are restless, lispy-voiced little beauties, but not so the ovenbird, or "teacher-bird," as it is often called in the back country. Though a true warbler, it is quite sedate, spending much of its time near or on the ground, customarily walking instead of hopping, and, in the case of a springtime male, frequently flying into a shrub or low tree branch to repeat its "tea*cher*, tea*cher*, tea*cher*, tea*cher*" refrain with astonishing vigor and in such increasing volume that the notes carry far through the warm May woods.

   This is the song that we usually hear, and it is a cheery, pleasant one indeed. But it is as nothing to the remarkable flight song which the male bird occasionally renders after sunset or during moonlit nights when, as though literally borne on the wings of music, he rises far above the treetops while he pours out an indescribable jumble of wild, ringing notes until, as though his lungs and fancy alike could do no more, he concludes with the familiar tea*cher,* tea*cher,* tea*cher* and drops back to the ground. Sometimes the performance is varied by flight through the woods instead of above them while singing, and a subdued version of the outburst from the branch of a tree is not at all uncommon.

Ovenbirds come north in rather early spring from their wintering grounds along the Gulf Coast, Central America, and Colombia, and from then until fall are well distributed through dryish woodlands from Alaska to Quebec and as far down as Arkansas, northern Georgia, and the Carolinas. Like the majority of birds, they are most noticeable during the nesting season, when the males put on a real show of singing, posturing, and crest-raising as they court their lady-loves.

The name ovenbird is singularly apt, for the typical nest is roofed over with an arch of dry leaves, grasses, bark strips, et cetera, and is provided with a side entrance, so that it somewhat resembles an old-fashioned brick oven. The first step is for both birds to round out a hollow in the ground, after which they start fashioning the dome-like cover. In two or three days, unless rain intervenes, the job is done, complete even to the soft lining of hair or fine grasses. Then come the eggs—four or five of them, creamy white spotted with reddish brown and lilac.

The female does most or all of the incubating—a rather risky task, as the nest's location directly on the ground subjects it to raids by all manner of woods prowlers. Of course the oven-like roof is good visual protection, and the mother bird takes full advantage of this by sitting so motionless and close that only the sharpest eyes could detect her. She will seldom leave her eggs until an intruder is almost near enough to step on nest and all, and then will try to entice the enemy from her treasures by feigning a broken wing as she totters and flutters away along the ground to what she considers a safe distance.

WATER-TURKEY

ECHO OF PREHISTORIC DAYS

There is more the appearance of snake than of turkey about this strange southern bird, though when its long tail is spread fanwise during flight it does suggest a gobbler's. Then, as you study the whole contour, especially the sinuous neck and head, you begin to wonder if the front end isn't descended from a snake and the rest from birds. There is a lot to be said for its other common names of snake-bird and black darter.

Water-turkeys measure about three feet from bill tip to the end of the noticeably long tail, and there is a thin fringe of longer feathers down the backs of their necks, suggestive of a short mane. The males are blackish with silvery patches on the front part of their wings, while the females and young are more brownish. Pink eyes surrounded by bare green skin, and sharp toenails on their webbed feet to assist them in climbing about among shrubs and trees, are finishing touches to a completely weird appearance.

This feathered anomaly is native to tropical America, occasionally found during the nesting season as far north as western Mexico, southern Illinois, and North Carolina. Its winters are spent in Florida and the Gulf States, and at any time of year the place to find it is cypress swamps, rice fields, and other wet places where there is plenty of good cover. Its stick and grass nest, containing two to five bluish or green eggs crusted over with white, is built in a bush or low tree, and there may be fifty or more pairs breeding in a single colony.

They are silent birds, these water-turkeys, rarely saying anything except the grating, harsh noises they make when alighting near their nests. Surprise them as they perch, cormorant-like, among the low branches, and they will drop noiselessly to the water, submerge

with scarcely a ripple, and swim away with only their heads and upper necks visible above the surface. Fish are their predominant food, and in the main the birds catch them by the simple, direct method of outswimming them under water.

For all their aquatic skill and tastes, water-turkeys are fast and capable fliers, sweeping through the air with alternate stretches of flapping and sailing, and often wheeling high in the blue after the fashion of hawks.

You would think that a bird capable of such air mastery would know how to land gracefully, but not the water-turkey. Instead it practically tumbles to its perch amid wild flappings and fumblings to catch its balance. Actually, most of the time water-turkeys seem to prefer sitting and swimming to flying, and often are unwilling to take wing even when you disturb them.

The snaky appearance of these peculiar birds is no mere matter of chance or imagination. Actually it demonstrates the fact that all birds are descended from reptiles and that the evolutionary process has altered some of them far less than others. According to the classifications determined by ornithologists, water-turkeys belong to one of the early or most primitive "orders"—in other words, groups that show relatively little change from their reptilian ancestors. Grebes and cormorants are other examples of retarded evolutionary progress, in contrast with the sparrows, which are rated as the most complex of all and farthest from reptiles in physical and other characteristics. In general, the early orders in the official check list of the American Ornithologists Union contain far fewer species than the later ones, which simply means that the great majority of our modern birds have come a long, long way from the likeness of their reptile forebears.

One naturally wonders why the water-turkey, for example, should have retained so much of its primitive nature while other birds were pressing ahead to higher stages of development. To my knowledge, there is no clear-cut explanation of such situations, other than that they are a part of the over-all plan of evolution. It may well be that the most primitive birds will eventually disappear, but that day will not come in your time or mine!

OSPREY

THE WHISTLING HAWK WITH MIGHTY WINGS

To most people a hawk is a more or less savage, big bird that eats poultry, birds, and other warm-blooded smaller creatures. A few of them are indeed like that, but generalizing about hawks is uncertain business, as the osprey, or fish hawk, clearly demonstrates.

These fish-eaters are really big fellows, with a wingspread sometimes as great as six feet (females only, as the males are almost always smaller), and weighing over four pounds. They are anything but savage, though, except in their defense of nest and young, and instead of screaming they sound a plaintive, shrill, quickly repeated whistle.

To carry their originality a bit farther, ospreys sometimes nest on such domesticated places as the roofs of fishermen's shacks, cartwheel platforms fastened on tall poles, and even farmhouse chimneys and the crossarms of telegraph poles. Usually the site they choose is high in a big and often dead tree, but whether or not it is far from a human habitation seems to be quite unimportant to its owners. In some coastal areas, where the birds are protected, they build right on the ground.

An osprey nest is a stupendous affair of branches, sticks, driftwood, cornstalks, seaweed, and what have you. The same pair will return to it year after year, adding more and more junk in their repairing operations until the whole mass ultimately weighs several hundred pounds and can be seen against the skyline for a mile or more. There are instances of small birds of several kinds nesting in the crevices of osprey castles, quite unmolested, which speaks well for the big fellows' tolerance.

These great hawks are expert fishermen, and their technique of capturing their prey is the essence of direct action. Flapping along fifty or more feet above the water, the bird spots a sizable swimmer fairly near the surface, closes its wings, plunges headfirst, and hits the water with such momentum that often it goes clear out of sight. Much more often than not it comes up with the fish clamped in its talons, rests an instant on the water, and then flaps up and away to feed the three or four kiddies, or itself, as the case may be.

And yet perhaps that last sentence about the fate of the fish should not stand unqualified, for if a bald eagle happens to be in the neighborhood it is likely to head for the fish hawk, beat it up by superior size and power, and force it to drop its booty, which the eagle then snatches for its own purposes. Yes, this is the same bald eagle that serves as our national emblem for all that is free and fair and noble!

Our race of ospreys is very widely distributed over North America during the breeding season, being found all the way from Alaska across to Labrador and southward to Lower California, the Gulf States, and Florida. In winter this range is extended still farther south through Mexico and into Central America and the West Indies. Other forms of the species live in Europe, most of Asia, the East Indies, Australia, and North Africa.

$\mathcal{R}$ING-NECKED $\mathcal{P}$HEASANT

FANTASY IN ORIENTAL COLORS

The oriental splendor of a cock ring-neck in full springtime plumage is beyond belief. Yellow bill, green head with black tufts like
little horns, bright red cheeks, a neckband of pure white, and below
that a superb and intricate pattern of iridescent browns, gold,
bronze, copper, gray, and black clear to the end of an incredibly
long-pointed tail—such is a purely factual outline of his color glory.
Display it all on a sturdy yet graceful form that may measure three
feet from bill tip to tail tip, and you have a magnificence that could
make even a peacock look to his laurels.

Actually this handsome game bird is of primarily Chinese origin
and so comes naturally by its Far Eastern gorgeousness. Many years
ago the breed was introduced in the United States and is now well
established in many areas from coast to coast and even lower

221

Canada. Hardy, prolific, and resourceful, it has adapted itself readily to our climatic conditions and to all intents and purposes has become a native American. To be sure, its excellence as a game and food bird makes it a prime favorite of hunters, but so many thousands are bred and raised in captivity for release in early autumn that the supply can be maintained. Thus our pheasant population is composed of both yard-hatched and wild-hatched birds.

Early in the spring, in that open, semicultivated country which ring-necks love so well, you will hear the cockbirds "crowing" to attract the attention of any females that may be in the neighborhood. Though their call is a far-reaching *kok-kok* rather than the barnyard rooster's *"cock-y-doodle-do,"* its character is definitely chicken-like, an impression heightened by the single wing clap which immediately precedes it and the short flutter that concludes the performance. Prior to actual mating a cock often "crows" every three or four minutes for an hour or so, then takes a short vacation before starting in again.

May and June are the nesting season, and the site selected is normally on the ground in brushy fields or pastures, woods edges, open moorlands or grainfields. The female, smaller and less colorful than the male but still a completely lovely creature, takes full charge of constructing the nest of dead leaves and grass to hold her six to fourteen olive-brown to pale bluish eggs and of incubating them for three or four weeks until they hatch. With so many to care for, she has to be especially careful to turn them at intervals so that all sides shall be directly exposed to the warmth of her body, a feat which she accomplishes by lowering her head and neck, slipping her bill under egg after egg and neatly rolling them over.

Like all fowl-like or gallinaceous birds, young ring-necks can run about as soon as they dry out after hatching, and then they and their mother leave the nest for good. From then on she leads them in the never-ending search for insects, seeds, and other pheasant foods, guarding them closely and marshaling them under her fluffed feathers at night until they grow too large to need that protection. By midsummer they are on the wing, and so a new generation of Far Eastern beauty takes its place in our American scene.

$\mathcal{C}$OMMON $\mathcal{S}$APSUCKER

IT DIGS ITS OWN WELLS IN TREES

Sapsuckers are members in good standing of the woodpecker tribe, but they are the only ones whose chisel strokes through the bark of trees are aimed primarily at getting sap to drink and soft sapwood to eat rather than insect larvae. Often a single individual will drill rows and rows of little wells around the trunk of some favorite tree and return to them at intervals for several days to collect nutritive dividends. In parts of the South considerable damage is done to timber trees in this way, and sapsuckers are considered real enemies by the owners of pecan orchards down that way. In the Northern States apple and pear trees are the prime favorites, but on a number of occasions I have seen cherry birches heavily scored with the unmistakable borings. Only last fall a single sapsucker haunted such a birch near my home for a full week, rarely leaving it even for an hour.

These active, self-assertive woodpeckers are noisy fellows, with a vocabulary that ranges from mews, whines, and clicks to loud squeals strongly suggestive of the blue jay and even the red-shouldered hawk. During the spring courting season the males sound a bit like a circus band, including the drums, which they simulate by beating on a dead tree branch or even a tin roof or metal eaves trough. One observer reports, apparently accurately, that he once found a sapsucker rapping on a tin dipper hung on a tree beside a spring.

And speaking of reports, the evidence appears to be conclusive that these rollicking birds sometimes get quite tight drinking tree sap that has fermented in the warm spring sun. No indication that they enjoy the experience, of course; it's just one of those things that happen by accident, so to speak.

The common sapsucker breeds from Newfoundland west to Alaska and south to southern California, New Mexico, Missouri, upland Virginia, Ohio, and New Hampshire. For the winter it moves south to lower New Jersey, Kansas, and on down as far as the West Indies and Central America. Thus, through the Northeast, we know it chiefly as a not too common but exceptionally interesting migrant. The birds are far more versatile in their diet than most other woodpeckers, for besides tree sap and inner bark and the insects attracted to them they pounce on many other insects after the manner of regular flycatchers and are fond of a variety of fruits, including the odd, pulpy red seed coverings of magnolias.

The nest, as with other woodpeckers, is in a cavity cut out by the birds in a dead tree, or occasionally in a living one. The gourd-shaped opening, reached by a two-inch hole at the top, is about a foot deep, and the six or seven white eggs are laid on the scattering of shreds and small chips in its concave bottom. There is usually only one clutch a year, and both parents share the duty of keeping the eggs warm for the two-week period required for hatching. Just to maintain the family reputation for oddities, the youngsters hiss like snakes while they're still in the nest.

All in all, sapsuckers are unusually interesting if not particularly appealing birds. They probably eat more vegetable food than they do animal matter, which puts them in a decidedly different dietary class than almost any other woodpecker. To facilitate this habit, their tongues have half brush-like rather than sharply pointed tips like those of other members of the group, and so are more efficient gatherers of sap and pulpy inner bark. In addition to this, the females, which wear crimson caps on their foreheads similar to their husbands', are unlikely to acquire this bit of finery until they are at least two years old. And as a final oddity, sapsuckers are fond of ants, spiders, and crickets, and are apparently able to eat poison-ivy berries without getting itchy stomachs. Yes, their acquaintance is well worth making, whenever opportunity arises.

$\mathcal{T}$REE $\mathcal{S}$PARROW

CHEERFUL THOUGH WINTER DOES ITS WORST

Why its first name should be "tree" is a minor mystery, for it spends most of the time on or near the ground, even building a typical bulky sparrow nest there in the Newfoundland, Labrador, and Hudson Bay regions which are its summer breeding ground. It would be far more appropriate to call these beautifully patterned little fellows "winter chipbirds," for here in the United States we see them only in the colder months, and at first glance they definitely resemble the chipping sparrow which is such a friendly and popular summer visitor in every dooryard.

Early October brings the first of the season's tree sparrows southward across the border, and by the beginning of winter they are widely distributed as far south as the Carolinas and westward to Arkansas and Oklahoma. Late February finds them heading north again, and by the end of April the last ones have vanished from sight but not from our thoughts, for they are among the most welcome of all our winter birds.

No weather seems too rough, no snow too deep for the cheery energy of these small northerners in their feather coats of bright browns, buffs, black pencilings and grays, topped by a broad crown band of brick red. They are forever on the go, foraging through the weedy fields, joining the juncos and black-capped chickadees at the feeding stations, staging harmless mock battles with their companions over grains and bread crumbs. They love to cling to a swaying weed or grass stalk, deftly snatching its seeds or harvesting

226

those which have fallen on the snow. Their consumption of this favorite food must be enormous; one authentic estimate places the total at 875 tons a year in a large agricultural state such as Iowa.

They are pleasantly talkative, too, especially when a group of them gathers in a wind-sheltered spot to feed or merely enjoy the sunshine. At such times they keep up a steady ice-fine twittering interspersed with *tseets* as thin as wire. Hearing them, you somehow think of dripping icicles, a similarity which becomes still sharper when, in late February and early March, their clear, tinkly songs begin.

$\mathscr{P}$ASSENGER $\mathscr{P}$IGEON

ITS MILLIONS ONCE FILLED THE SKY

Once upon a time, before white men took over America, the graceful "wild pigeon" was believed to be the most abundant bird in the world, blanketing the northern half of the states east of the Great Plains in spring and summer and the lower half in winter. Nearly eighteen inches long, handsome in pastel shades of blue, gray, rose, and brown, it swept across the sky in immense flocks that sometimes contained billions of birds, literally blotting out the sun for hours during their passage. When they gathered to roost for the night the multitudes broke great limbs from forest trees with the sheer weight of their numbers, and the sound of their wings and the tumult of their settling could be heard for miles. Each pair built three or four flimsy twig nests a year, containing one or two eggs apiece, and some of their forest breeding colonies were known to have been as much as forty miles long and seven wide, with countless trees carrying fifty or more nests. As the grown birds fed along the ground (their diet included beechnuts, chestnuts, insects, wild berries, seeds, and grain) they looked like a constantly breaking soft blue wave, rolling steadily forward as those in the rear flew low over their companions and settled in front of them.

Yes, it well could have been the world's most abundant bird. Yet

228

today it is the opinion of competent authorities that not one passenger pigeon remains alive.

Many theories have been advanced for the "sudden" disappearance of these incredible hordes of strong, swift-flying birds: cutting down of their forest homes, mysterious pestilence, catastrophic loss by storm as they flew across the Gulf of Mexico, and so on. None of these explanations, however, stands up under careful scrutiny as a major factor. The real reason was our own monstrous wastage of the abundance of our land, a story of human indifference and greed so insatiable that today it seems hardly credible.

We began our mass killing of passenger pigeons in New England within fifty years after the Pilgrims landed at Plymouth Rock, and continued it for more than two centuries. Year after year their dense nesting and roosting colonies were subjected to organized raids that employed every imaginable method of killing—guns, fire, clubs, long poles, suffocating clouds of sulphur smoke, even heavy swivel guns loaded with handfuls of shot. In open country the feeding grounds were baited and huge nets were spread so that they could be dropped over the hungry birds and catch as many as three hundred at a time. Regular companies were formed to market the dead birds; whole schoonerloads used to come down the Hudson River to be sold in New York City at twelve to fifty cents a dozen, depending on the season. In the year 1848 eighty tons of pigeon carcasses were shipped from a single county in New York State. At one Michigan nesting site one hundred barrels, each containing forty dozen bodies, were shipped every day for a month.

Gradually the pigeon multitudes were driven westward, harried constantly wherever they went. Many crossed the border into Canada, with the market hunters hard on their trail. By 1890 the flocks had been so decimated that market hunting practically ceased; there appears to be no authentic record of even a single bird having been taken in the wild since 1898. And on September 1, 1914, the very last passenger pigeon, so far as we know, died in the Cincinnati Zoological Garden at the age of at least eleven years. It was the lone survivor of a small flock bred and raised in captivity from a single pair owned and cared for by Professor C. O. Whitman of Chicago.

PUFFIN

A SERIOUS CLOWN IN HARLEQUIN CLOTHES

A single glimpse of an adult puffin in breeding plumage is enough to make you wonder what sort of drollery Nature was up to when she designed such a grotesque little feathered buffoon. Dumpy, pompous in pose, and with its black and white costume set off by red splayfeet and an enormous tricolor bill of yellow, gray-blue, and vermilion, it looks like something out of the Sunday colored "funnies" in those days when the youth of our land was more interested in fantasy than ferocity. Furthermore, puffins are nearly as comical in actions as in looks, as the late Edward Howe Forbush so perfectly wrote in *Birds of Massachusetts and Other New England States:*

"On the wing the puffin buzzes about as if upon important business. It tumbles out of its hole, flies down and into the sea, flies around under water, flies out again, and here it comes back to the rocks, its great 'red nose' pointing the way, its little saber-like wings beating the air like a threshing machine and its red feet spread out behind. When it comes up from the depths to find that it is being overtaken by a steamboat it is very likely to lose its head and show the most comical kind of apprehension and indecision. It dips its head under water as if to dive, then raises it and tries to fly, gives this up and finally dives through a wave, comes flying out on the other side and dives again until finally it has blundered and floundered out of the way. When under water it seems to use its wings mainly for progression and its feet chiefly for steering, as it does when flying in the air."

Puffins breed on islands off the Atlantic Coast from Greenland to Maine and spend the winter out at sea in the same general latitudes

and occasionally as far south as upper Massachusetts. On their chosen nesting sites they gather in colonies and dig burrows two feet or so long into sloping banks, at the ends of which they assemble some dead grass and sometimes a few feathers by way of nest. There is but one new generation a year, and usually the female lays only a single white, vaguely marked egg, though sometimes she is ambitious enough to make it two. She and her husband share the incubation chores, and it is he that does most of the original burrowing. So, for all his ludicrous appearance, a papa puffin does have his practical, serious side.

It must be rather boring to sit at the end of a long, dark tunnel underground for hours at a time. Nesting puffins apparently find it so, for when one comes out after an incubation session it stretches and flutters its wings as if grateful to get out into the air. Don't think for a moment, though, that these foot-long clowns take their home duties lightly. Were you to be so foolhardy as to reach your hand into a burrow when one of its owners is there, you would regret it, for a nesting puffin can and will bite and scratch like fury.

$\mathscr{B}$LACKBURNIAN $\mathscr{W}$ARBLER

HE WEARS THE SUN'S GLOW ON HIS BREAST

Wood warblers as a whole are widely noted for their bright and contrasting dress, covering literally all the colors of the rainbow; but of the fifty-odd kinds which constitute the family, the blackburnian is the most startlingly brilliant. When you see the May sun glinting on the flame-orange throat and upper breast of a male in full plumage you can hardly believe that such a glowing, vital hue can be held in a few small feathers. The same gorgeous color is echoed on the forehead and cheeks, where it is accentuated by an intervening pattern of black, while the rest of the upper parts are strikingly black and white. Curiously enough, the spring markings of the female are almost identical with those of the male, although their colors are less vividly and stunningly displayed.

From Peru and the Guianas to Maine and Ontario is a long trip for a five-inch bird, but the blackburnians take it every spring and retrace their course in the fall. Between these two seasons they contrive to raise families of perhaps four little blackburnians each, in twig, rootlet, and moss nests often high among the evergreen trees of Canada, the northern tier of states, and southward through the mountains to the Carolinas. Perhaps they need the comparative rest they find in their South American winter resort!

Most of us know these flaming beauties only occasionally, if at all, as they pass through in migration, for in most areas and during most years they seem none too common. Perhaps one reason for their apparent scarcity is that they prefer the tall treetops to the lower growth, and so are among the most difficult warblers to identify under average conditions. Your best chance for a really good look at them comes when a sharp drop in temperature during the peak of the spring migration forces them, together with many other tree-haunting birds, to seek their insect food at lower levels. Then, if you are fortunate enough to come upon one of the small local concentrations which not infrequently occur in early May, you will be treated to a sight to be remembered for many a year.

By late August they are moving south again, and the males' burning orange has lightened and the bright black markings on the upper plumage have dulled. At this season there is little to choose between the costumes of the old and young birds, regardless of their sex. Only an experienced observer, indeed, can tell them apart, and to most of us they are just some more pretty little warblers journeying to warmer regions for the winter.

$\mathscr{D}$OWNY $\mathscr{W}$OODPECKER

SMALL, BUT WHAT A PERSONALITY!

The downy is our smallest American woodpecker, but if you accept that old Scottish saying about the best goods coming in small packages, it rates very high indeed. Into the six to seven inches which comprise its over-all length it packs a world of personality. Friendly, independent, amusing, energetic, playful, and at times downright seriocomic, its change of pace is astonishing. At any moment it may become either a clown or a philosopher.

Downies are year-round residents from Newfoundland to Alaska and southward to the Gulf Coast. Throughout this vast area they are stand-bys of bird-feeding people, seeming never to tire of a diet of fresh suet. Last winter five of them—three red-capped males and two more soberly dressed females—came constantly to my Connecticut feeding stations, and when, after much ludicrous springtime courting and battling, a match was concluded between two of them, the pair chipped a nesting hole out of a nearby tree stub and in due course brought their four children to introduce them to the handouts which were still on hand. We never had more courteous and entertaining guests.

All true woodpeckers, of course, live primarily on insect larvae, ants, and eggs, which they gather from or beneath the bark of trees, shrubs, or even large non-woody plants by banging away with chisel-pointed bills until they have hammered a hole that enables them to pull out the victim with their long, spear-pointed tongues. In the case of the little downy, especially, this rugged procedure makes you wonder how the bird ever escapes having a perpetual headache from the concussion of its blows. This feeding technique, though, is nothing compared to the triphammer drumming of a male on a dead limb as he challenges a possible rival or advertises for a wife when the mating season nears. Often he will move from limb to limb and spot to spot, testing each, until he finds one whose tone exactly strikes his fancy.

Spending as much time as they do among the upper branches of large trees, you would think that these little black and white fellows would fall easy prey to hawks when the falling of the leaves deprives them of all concealment. But downies have a simple answer to that one: they merely dodge around to the opposite side of the trunk or branch when they see a hawk coming. If he still persists, they can and will play hide-and-seek much faster than he can— and almost always get away with it. Often, if a downy happens to be on a more or less horizontal branch when danger threatens, it will flatten itself motionless on the under side for minutes at a time. When it thinks the coast is clear it will reconnoiter cautiously and with complete calmness until safety is assured, and then go on about its business as though nothing had happened.

This sort of agile tree life calls for special equipment, and the downy has that too—feet whose four strong toes can be spread in any direction for the best possible grip, and pointed, stiff-tipped tail feathers which serve as highly efficient props to help hold their owner in place on the often vertical bark.

237